GREAT
SCOTT

KEN KISTER

GREAT SCOTT

THERE'S AN ÜBER RIGHT-WING CREEP IN THE FLORIDA GOVERNOR'S OFFICE;

OR HOW RICK SCOTT AND THE REPUBLICAN-DOMINATED FLORIDA LEGISLATURE SHAFTED JUST ABOUT EVERYONE IN THE SUNSHINE STATE FROM

JANUARY 2011 TO APRIL 2012—EXCEPT CORPORATIONS AND THE VERY RICH

Gov. Scotts ALTERNATIVE TO HIGH SPEED RAIL LINKING TAMPA TO ORLANDO.

CONTENTS

Politics is perhaps the only profession for which no preparation is thought necessary.

——Robert Louis Stevenson, *Familiar Studies of Men and Books*

AUTHOR'S INTRODUCTION

Although I've been interested in politics for many years, I do not have a degree in political science, nor am I a political insider, nor have I ever seriously worked on a political campaign. Likewise, I am not an academician nor an investigative journalist. Rather, I'm a natural born U.S. citizen who lives and works in Florida as a freelance writer who is very much alarmed by the actions and attitudes of ultraconservative elected officials such as Rick Scott, Florida's current governor.

Sad to say, the American rightwing has been on the march recently, its leaders eager to systematically dismantle progressive laws and programs that have improved the lives of a great many Americans over the years. Victims of this movement include the nation's vast but shrinking middle class, which comprises a broad range of hardworking people, some of whom wear white collars, others blue collars. Whatever the color or cut of their uniform, middle-class people historically have been the muscle, backbone, and heart and soul of the nation. Other victims are America's underclass: the poor, the unemployed, the homeless, the disabled, the sick. These vulnerable citizens, whose numbers are increasing at a disturbing rate, are often the first targets of regressive political action simply because they are weak and normally lack the wherewithal to resist.

The fact is today hard-core conservative office holders at all levels of government, aided by wealthy corporatist sponsors, are relentlessly gnawing away like rats at the foundations of the economic and social progress that over the years have made the United States a strong and buoyant democracy. Fueled by hubris and untold supplies of money for political smear campaigns, these callous power brokers use a variety of deceitful tactics to hoodwink many Americans into voting against their self-interest—or not voting at all. A prominent example is the Big Lie, a technique perfected by Joseph Goebbels, Nazi Germany's official propagandist, that postulates if a lie is told often enough—and bold and loud enough—it becomes The Truth, at least for some. Think "Willie Horton." Think "Swift Boat." Think "Death Panels." Think "Class Warfare." Think the sneering, constantly repeated negative references to "Obamacare."

In 2011 Rick Scott and the Republican majority in the Florida Legislature used the Big Lie to enact a new election law allegedly designed to put a stop to "voter fraud" in the state. Nonpartisan investigators, however, have found only a few cases of such fraud reported in Florida in recent years; in fact, during the four-year period 2008 to 2011, there have been more shark attacks in Florida than instances of voter fraud. The real intent of the new law, it seems apparent, is to suppress or discourage turnout by likely Democratic voters, such as African Americans, Hispanics, college students, and people who rely on Social Security, Medicare, Medicaid, and other entitlements. Entitlements, by the way, are entitled because they have either been earned by working people or are provided by a compassionate society to assist those unable to work.

It's heartening, therefore, that more and more citizens are awakening to the dangers posed by the radical right and are beginning to fight back. Indeed, if the mass of Americans do not fight back expeditiously and energetically, the ideologies and tactics espoused by hard-right extremists will in time destroy democracy in America, leaving in its wake a venal plutocracy. Or as former U.S. Supreme Court Justice Louis Brandeis once famously observed, "We may have democracy, or we may have wealth concentrated in the hands of a few, but we cannot have both."

This book, then, is in the broadest sense a j'accuse, a citizen's complaint against current efforts by obscenely wealthy corporatists to further enrich and empower the few at the expense of the many.

As noted, the focus in the book is on one particular elected official, Rick Scott, a corporatist who used his own fortune—at least some of which appears to have been accrued through, shall we say, dubious means—to buy the governorship of Florida in 2010. Derisively titled *Great Scott*, the book describes Scott's unexpected rise to political power in Florida, and then examines in some detail how he dealt with major issues impacting the state during his first 16 months as governor. In sum, the book is a grim chronicle of how Rick Scott, in concert with a largely compliant Republican-controlled state Legislature, created a lot of dark days in the Sunshine State

Ken Kister
Tampa, Florida
July 2012

ACKNOWLEDGMENTS

This book is significantly enhanced by Vanessa Montenegro's original political cartoons that appear on the cover and within its pages. A graphic artist, Ms. Montenegro lives, creates, and teaches art in Tampa, Florida.

Likewise, thanks are due to friend Paul Wetmore for his much valued assistance concerning computer technology, for which I have no facility.

ILLUSTRATIONS

RICK SCOTT IN CARTOON MODE

-1-

SCOTT'S LIFE BEFORE FLORIDA, 1952-2003.

Richard Lynn "Rick" Scott was born in Bloomington. Illinois, on December 1, 1952, into a lower middle-class family who lived in public housing. His father, who was periodically unemployed, worked as a bus and truck driver; his mother, a strict parent, had various jobs, mainly clerking at retail stores such as J.C. Penney. The Scotts were Methodists who believed in hard work and basic Christian values, and their five children, including Rick, were raised to abide by these precepts; if backsliding occurred, the paddle was an option. On the positive side, as Rick grew up he always impressed people as an extremely hard worker, and one colleague who knew him after he became a big success in the healthcare industry remembered that, even when provoked, Rick "didn't curse." On the flip side, Scott sometimes has difficulty telling the truth; he also has a penchant for evasiveness and secrecy, and a tendency not always to live up to the Eighth of the Ten Commandments.

Young Rick graduated from high school in 1970, after which he attended community college for a short time before enlisting in the U.S. Navy, where he served for more than two years, receiving an honorable discharge in 1974. While in the Navy he married Ann, the apple of his eye in high school. Over the course of their marriage, they have had two daughters, Jordan and Allison, and today Ann Scott is the first lady of Florida.

After leaving the Navy, he studied at the University of Missouri—Kansas City, using the GI Bill to earn an undergraduate degree in business administration. While in college, Scott, who quickly gained a reputation as a young man in a big hurry, worked full-time at a local grocery store. Also at this time he got his first taste of the world of entrepreneurship when he and his wife bought two doughnut shops in a downscale area of Kansas City. The experience, assisted by Rick's mother who managed the shops, proved to be both profitable and edifying. Next, he was off to Southern Methodist University in Dallas, Texas, to study law. After receiving his degree and passing the bar, he joined Johnson & Swanson, at the time the largest law firm in Dallas. Eventually he became a partner specializing in healthcare mergers and acquisitions.

In 1987, while still at Johnson & Swanson, Scott, now 35, began his intense involvement in the business of acquiring for-profit hospitals, which had two primary goals: first, to make money for himself and his partners; and second, to make hospitals more cost-efficient and better managed than their not-for-profit counterparts, mostly operated by universities and charities. This eventful part of Scott's early career turned out to be a roller-coaster ride that in a relatively short time would take him to the pinnacle of the U.S. healthcare world—and then abruptly to its nadir.

It started with typical Scott business bravado. He and a couple of well-heeled investors put together a $6 billion offer (with Citicorp providing financing) to purchase the Hospital Corporation of America (HCA), a large, nationally respected hospital chain headquartered in Nashville, Tennessee. Dr. Thomas Frist Jr., HCA's CEO, rejected the deal out of hand, but Scott was not deterred, sensing he was onto something that one day could make him a rich man. The next year he and Texas billionaire Richard Rainwater, an investment manager who also happened to be on the HCA board, each put up $125,000 to form a new company called Columbia Healthcare Corporation. This was a huge gamble for Scott, as $125,000 represented his and his wife's total life savings at the time. He immediately went to work, sending out letters to hundreds of U.S. hospitals, inquiring about their availability for acquisition or joint ventures. Not long after that, Columbia, with Scott negotiating every detail, purchased two financially stressed hospitals in El Paso, Texas, for $60 million. Within a year the El Paso hospitals were doing much better under Columbia's management, and the ambitious Scott was off and running. Between 1989 and 1993, Columbia added 92 more hospitals to its rapidly growing chain.

In 1994 Scott was finally able to get his hands on HCA in a merger deal with the Nashville-based company that then owned 96 hospitals. With Columbia's 94, he now presided over a grand total of 190 for-profit hospitals in the U.S. with annual revenues of roughly $11 billion. At this point Columbia Healthcare changed its name to Columbia/HCA, and the national press began referring to the 42-year-old Scott as America's "Hospital Czar." And as he continued to gobble up more and more hospitals and related medical facilities, Columbia/HCA became known in medical circles, according to one observer, as "a corporate eating machine." By 1996 Scott's empire was the largest, most dominant for-profit healthcare provider in the U.S., perhaps the world, the publicly traded chain now boasting more than 340 hospitals, 130 surgery centers, and an estimated 550 home health facilities with locations in 38 states and a couple of foreign countries. With revenues exceeding $23 billion a year, it ranked among the top one hundred companies in the universe.

Rick Scott by this time was also on top of the world. From two crummy doughnut shops in Kansas City to this! In interviews he radiated corporate swagger. He, a boy from public housing, had the American Dream by the tail. Of course there were naysayers and nagging signs that not all was completely copacetic, that Scott's push for profits might have led to skirting or ignoring a federal regulation or two here and there, but didn't everyone in the business do that? Well, no, apparently not everyone took such a laissez faire attitude toward cutting corners. For instance, when Columbia/HCA pushed for a merger deal with the Helen Ellis Memorial Hospital in Tarpon Springs, Florida, a knowledgeable community activist spoke up, comparing Scott's hospital chain to "a pack of great white sharks." Also, disquieting scuttlebutt circulated that the feds were digging around looking for irregularities concerning the way Columbia conducted its business.

But nothing ever seemed to come of these warning signs, so why worry? Likewise, there were expressions of concern by some within the Columbia family, including board vice chairman Tom Frist, who when HCA merged with Columbia joined the company's board of directors. Frist sensed that Scott's aggressive tactics and hard-nosed attitude toward treatment of hospital patients hurt the company's image. For example, Scott was quoted in an article in *The Nation* (November 18, 1996) on the subject of medicine as a profit-making venture as saying, "Do we [for-profit hospitals] have an obligation to provide health care for everybody? Where do we draw the line? Is any fast-food restaurant obligated to feed everyone who shows up?" Some felt this unfeeling remark and others like it went beyond a simple public relations gaffe.

Still, why worry. A few months earlier, *Time* magazine (June 17, 1996) had profiled Scott, praising his for-profit philosophy: "Scott's credo is a classic: quality care doesn't have to come at a premium price. But it's the way Scott is accomplishing that goal that is transforming how American hospitals do business. In an industry notorious for waste and inefficiency, Scott aggressively consolidates operations and imposes cost controls."

But shortly thereafter, with little real warning, Scott's image as a miracle worker began to crumble . . . and crumble quickly.

On March 19, 1997 the U.S. government, in a coordinated effort involving the FBI, IRS, Department of Health and Human Services, and several other federal agencies, began the operational phase of an extensive, well-planned, multi-state probe of Columbia/HCA's business culture, concentrating on Medicare and Medicaid fraud, but not limited to these specific programs. Hospitals and doctors' offices were raided, their books seized, and personnel interrogated by officials looking for evidence of criminality. Initially conceived in 1994, the investigation would not be concluded until early 2003, when Columbia (now called HCA, Inc.) paid a final fine of $631 million. All told, over a period of nearly ten years, more than 500 federal agents worked on this historic case.

It didn't take long for the story to go viral in the summer of 1997. In mid-July, warrants were served in Florida, North Carolina, Oklahoma, Tennessee, Texas, and Utah. In Tampa, Florida, John Fitzgibbons, an attorney who represented medical personnel and companies being investigated by government agencies, told the *Tampa Tribune* (July 17, 1997) that the probe was just getting started, that Columbia/HCA's business practices represented "the forefront of massive federal criminal activity in the health care field." Fitzgibbons further noted, "There's a small army of agents and prosecutors out there." On July 25 Scott and his number two, David Vandewater, were forced to resign from Columbia/HCA., leaving Tom Frist to clean up the mess. Three weeks later, New York state comptroller Carl McCall told the press that federal indictments had exposed a "corporate culture of criminal activity" at the giant hospital chain. Two years later, Columbia/HCA changed its name to HCA, Inc.

By 2000 the case was still in the courts, but the dimensions of the scandal could now be clearly laid out for all to see, including medical consumers and American taxpayers, both of whom had been defrauded by an avaricious corporation. Among the numerous media accounts, Dan Ackman's in the December 15, 2000 issue of *Forbes* magazine offers an especially good summary of the illegalities involved:

"Yesterday, the nation's largest hospital chain, known until recently as Columbia/ HCA, pleaded guilty to a variety of fraud charges. It admitted to bilking various government programs and agreed to pay a total of $840 million in fines and penalties. The fraud settlement is the largest in U.S. history . . . .

"The guilty plea follows a seven-year federal investigation that resulted in charges being filed in five different federal courts in Florida, Texas, Georgia and Tennessee . . . . The fraud revealed by that investigation ran deep within HCA's [i.e., Columbia/HCA's] way of doing business. Speaking at a news conference yesterday, U.S. Attorney General Janet Reno said about the plea deal, 'It's a simple message—if you overbill the U.S. taxpayer, we're going to make you pay it back, and then some.'

"The company admitted to systematically overcharging the government by claiming marketing costs as reimbursable, by striking illegal deals with home care agencies, and by filing false data about how hospital space was being used.

"The company increased Medicare billings by exaggerating the seriousness of the illnesses they were treating. It also granted doctors partnerships in company hospitals as a kickback for the doctors referring patients to HCA [i.e., Columbia/HCA]. In addition, it gave doctors 'loans' that were never expected to be paid back, free rent, free office furniture, and free drugs from hospital pharmacies.

"The investigation and the plea is an obvious blow to a company that became a Wall Street darling by promising to bring first-class business practices to the hospital sector, still dominated by not-for-profits. Under former Chief Executive Richard Scott, it bought hospitals by the bucketful and promised to squeeze blood from each one."

Later, in 2002 *The New York Times* (December 18) reported that some internal Columbia/HCA documents were "stamped with warnings that they should not be disclosed to Medicare auditors."

By the time the federal government wrote finis to this monster case in 2003, HCA had shelled out more than $2 billion to cover the costs of fines, penalties, and legal fees. It was, and remains today, one of the largest and arguably most disconcerting fraud cases in U.S. history. In addition to the financial cost to the company, a number of Columbia/HCA employees were indicted and tried, some were found guilty, and at least a few sentenced to prison.

And what about Richard Lynn "Rick" Scott? The man most responsible for creating, managing, and growing Columbia/HCA. What sort of retribution was meted out to this hard-driving lawyer who cofounded the company and was its longtime hands-on president and CEO? Most casual observers would say, well, he must have been one of those few who was indicted, convicted, and sent to prison. Remember *Time* magazine's glowing profile of Scott in 1996? Well, a little more than a year later, after the scandal broke, the magazine profiled the real Scott in its August 4, 1997 issue, putting him on its list of all-time entrepreneurial scammers. He was now portrayed as a "headstrong, self-centered manager" who "regards anyone who is not totally for him as the enemy." *Time* further noted that Scott had a "take-no-prisoners arrogance that alienates others." And "In the end, Scott's hubris may have cost him his empire . . . . Scott's refusal to consider—much less negotiate—a possible settlement was in keeping with his pugnacious stance on health-care administration. As head of Columbia, Scott demanded that acquired hospitals hit relentlessly ambitious profit targets year after year, raising concerns in some quarters about the quality of the medical care that patients were receiving." This is damning stuff, and many other respected media sources were saying similar things about the former "hospital czar."

Surely the feds <u>must</u> have nailed this guy.

But would you believe, Scott did not go to jail, nor was he acquitted or convicted because, incredibly, <u>he was never charged with any culpability</u> in the Columbia/HCA case. Rather, he claimed absolute ignorance of any wrongdoing. After his forced resignation, he lamented, "Oh, if only someone told me something was wrong." By Scott's version of the events, not only was he innocent but, poor Rick, he had been let down by underlings! Happily for him, his hurt feelings were more than a little assuaged by his generous golden parachute, a settlement amounting to almost $10 million. He also departed Columbia/HCA with shares in the company worth in excess of $300 million. It's tempting to say sometimes crime does pay.

Here's the problem: When Scott was the top executive at Columbia, he was widely recognized as a very smart, very experienced attorney-cum-businessman working at the highest levels of corporate America and a man who prided himself on his "attention to detail." If one believes he knew nothing about the criminal culture uncovered at Columbia, then Scott either has the IQ of a bedpan or he was not telling the truth. Carl Hiaasen, a writer who has one of Florida's wickedest pens, put it this way in an October 2010 *Miami Herald* column: "If he [Scott] truly didn't know what was happening all around him, he's an incompetent fool. And if he did know, he's a lying crook."

The question remains, why was Rick Scott never deposed, charged, prosecuted, and sentenced to prison for his role in the epic Columbia/HCA debacle? No one except for a few government insiders knows the answer for certain. Everyone else is left to guess. The author of this book guesses—indeed, has a strong suspicion—that Scott got a pass because he was too big and too rich and too well-connected to prosecute. Although it's regrettable, in this country all too often top corporate executives strongly suspected of white-collar crime are let off the hook. This appears to be what happened in the Columbia/HCA case, where the only people who were held accountable for the widespread corruption were relatively small fish who worked for a big shark. Or it might simply have been that the Justice Department felt it did not have enough hard evidence to win in the courtroom against Scott, who obviously had more than ample resources to buy the best defense lawyers available.

After Scott resigned from Columbia/HCA in 1997 with a tarnished reputation but comforted by that multimillion dollar severance package, he did not hide, or retire, or go into a blue funk, or spend time having conscience-stricken regrets. That is not Rick Scott's style. Rather, he carried on as if nothing had happened, continuing his habit of developing and acquiring businesses. For instance, later that year, he founded Richard L. Scott Investments, LLC, a private equity firm that has holdings in companies representing a variety of industries, including healthcare. In 1998, he bought a majority share in an around-the-clock TV cable channel called America's Health Network that later became The Health Network and later still Discovery Health. In 2001, he cofounded Solantic, a chain of for-profit emergency care clinics that furnish basic medical services. In 2003, he invested roughly $5 million in Pharmaca Integrative Pharmacies, a company devoted to servicing drugstores and other retail outlets that sell herbal and homeopathic products.

Also in 2003 the Scott family moved to Florida, settling in Naples, a community located in the southwestern part of the state between the Everglades and the Gulf of Mexico. It's doubtful if at this time Scott, now 50 years old, had any plans, specific or vague, for a political career—that would have taken some really big cojones after the disgraceful Columbia/HCA scandal. But it wouldn't take him too long to develop the itch.

2

HE MOVES TO FLORIDA IN 2003 AND RUNS FOR GOVERNOR IN 2010

Naples, seat of Florida's Collier County, is a small, upscale city of roughly 22,000 people, the majority of whom are politically conservative and financially well off. In fact, little Naples probably has as many millionaires per square inch as, say, Palm Beach or Sarasota, which are among Florida's best known havens for the very rich. Certainly when the Scotts came to Naples in 2003, there was no doubt they, ensconced in their $9 million home, would fit in quite nicely. Rick and Ann immediately began supporting local civic projects and charities, and soon got involved in building a new church. Naturally Rick continued working diligently on business matters, now as a "venture capitalist," an unofficial title that replaced the previous "hospital czar." All of this—new home, new city, new state, new vocational challenge—kept Scott busy, busy for the next five years.

Then something happened that would change Rick Scott's life: Barak Obama was elected president of the United States in November 2008.

During Obama's first two years as president, his number one priority, as he had promised during the campaign, was passage of legislation to reform the country's broken healthcare system—a system that excluded millions of citizens, that was susceptible to large-scale fraud (as Scott knew oh so well), and whose costs were spiraling out of control.

Scott, an ultraconservative Republican who believes fiercely in such shibboleths as "free enterprise," "unfettered capitalism," "privatization," and of course "for-profit," was both appalled and incensed by Obama's policies. After all, he, Rick Scott, was a man who not so long ago had headed a formidable medical enterprise built on the for-profit principle. Now, here was this new president of the United States, a former "community organizer," scheming to "nationalize" the way the country's population receives and pays for its healthcare. It was, at least in the minds of hard-core political conservatives like Scott, a dastardly attempt to impose "socialized medicine," that old bugaboo, on the American people.

Scott's first instinct was to lobby forcefully against the president's proposed legislation, and he did just that. In early 2009, he created a national advocacy group called Conservatives for Patients' Rights, or CPR, investing approximately $5 million to jump-start the organization and to hire a public relations outfit called Creative Response Concepts, which previously had worked on such projects as the Swift Boat ads that helped jettison John Kerry's presidential bid. Scott made it clear that others, not he, would be the public face of CPR, telling associates, "I would just as soon not be in the limelight" (*Gulf Coast Business Review,* March 26, 2009).

But little more than a year later, Rick Scott would be chasing the limelight like the moth the star.

What no one knew in early 2009—certainly not Scott—was that a confluence of decisions by two eminent Florida office holders would fundamentally alter the state's political landscape going into the 2010 elections. By the time election day had rolled around in November, the careers of <u>three</u> prominent state politicians would be in tatters. Conversely, a long-shot Cuban-American state legislator from Miami named Marco Rubio would emerge as Florida's junior U.S. senator. Even more surprising, a tall, gangly, bald man with a highly suspicious background, who had lived in the state for only a short time and who was completely unknown to the vast majority of Floridians six months prior to the election, would become Florida's 45th governor. That man, of course, was Rick Scott.

How this improbable scenario occurred will be told time and again in Florida history books. Suffice it to say here that it all began in late 2008 when Mel Martinez, Republican U.S. senator from Florida and the first Cuban American to serve in that august body, announced he would not run for reelection in 2010, even though he had yet to serve one full six-year term. Martinez claimed he was disillusioned with Washington politics, but others wondered if his real ambition was to become a lobbyist, which paid a heck of lot more money than being a senator. Whatever the reason, Martinez's decision set off a game of political musical chairs that would keep a host of Florida politicians and their strategists busy recalibrating plans right up to election day on November 2, 2010.

Charlie Crist, the state's popular Republican governor, who had been elected to a four-year term in 2006, was the first to make a move. On May 12, 2009 he indicated he would not run for reelection as governor in 2010 as had been expected, but instead would seek Martinez's vacant seat in the U.S. Senate. Then, after appointing a loyal minion to keep the senate seat warm until he could assume it, Crist sat back to watch the game, secure in the certain knowledge that his high poll numbers would easily carry him to the nation's capital the following year. A handsome, well-tailored man, Crist always looked ahead to the next rung on the political ladder. He had started in the Florida Legislature in 1992 as a hard-right conservative, best known as "Chain Gang Charlie" for his advocacy of tough prison reforms. In recent years, however, he had adopted a much more moderate stance while serving as the state's education commissioner, then attorney general, and now governor, believing that voters were looking for politicians who understood the value of bipartisanship in the political process. Indeed, in February 2009 Gov. Crist appeared with Barak Obama at a rally in Fort Myers, Florida, promoting the president's economic stimulus program. To show his support, Republican Crist gave the Democratic president a "man-hug." Also, in 2008 Crist had actively backed John McCain's bid for the Republican presidential nomination, hoping quite openly that he might be picked as McCain's running mate should the old soldier win the nomination.

With Charlie Crist no longer running for a second term as governor, a familiar Florida Republican face, Bill McCollum, jumped into the race for that office, making his announcement on May 18, just a week after Crist had opted for the U.S. Senate. At the time, McCollum was Florida's attorney general (or AG) and was well-known around the state due to previously serving in the U.S. House of Representatives for 20 years (1981-2001) and running statewide twice, first losing the Republican nomination for U.S. Senate in 2004 to Mel Martinez (remember him?), and then more recently winning his current position as AG. As is the case with most politicians who have been around the block a time or two, McCollum brought a certain amount of baggage to the governor's race, including being pilloried by critics for his snarky conduct during the Bill Clinton impeachment business back in the late 1990s when McCollum was one of the Republican leaders in the U.S. House, and later while Florida's AG for bungling an investigation concerning the emotional issue of gay adoption. Despite such negatives, the Florida Republican establishment embraced McCollum as its presumptive nominee for governor. Though not an exciting candidate, he was a safe choice, an experienced pol who normally wouldn't veer too far off GOP talking points. Besides, most pundits at the time picked McCollum as the odds on favorite to beat anyone the Democrats nominated for governor.

During this period of intense political jockeying, Rick Scott, venture capitalist, watched developments unfold with keen interest.

Though new to Florida and only superficially familiar with the state's political institutions and personalities, he was not naive about politicians as a species. As CEO of Columbia/HCA for ten years, Scott had doubtless rubbed shoulders with thousands of so-called public servants at all levels of government in many different places, including Florida where Columbia owned dozens of hospitals and other healthcare facilities. Martinez's unexpected rejection of life in the U.S. Senate, and Crist's unexpected decision to trade the governor's mansion in Tallahassee (the state's capital) for a possible sinecure in Washington D.C., did not surprise him in the least. On the other hand, these events did change everything.

True, not that long ago, Scott had told his CPR organization that he didn't want to be in the limelight, and probably at the time he meant it. But now, with the Columbia/HCA scandal pretty much pushed into the background of the general public's short memory, and with the popular Crist very much out of the way, it occurred to him that it might be an opportune time for someone else—perhaps the ever-ambitious Rick Scott himself?—to make a bid for the governor's office. Think of it, as governor he would be considerably more effective marshaling strong opposition to President Obama's healthcare reform legislation than pulling strings behind the scenes at CPR. As wheels turned, new configurations required new evaluations.

However, before Scott could do anything concerning a possible run for governor, he had to find out what the residency requirement was for Florida gubernatorial candidates and then determine if he met the requirement. As it turned out, state law mandates candidates for governor must have lived in Florida for a minimum of seven years, and by golly, as luck would have it, Scott just qualified, having now lived in Naples for seven years plus a few weeks to spare. The next step was to sit down with trusted friends and advisers, including wife Ann, and weigh the pros and cons of getting into the race. Details of exactly how all of this unfolded and who said what to whom when and where is not public knowledge, but surely the following issues and concerns must have been addressed in some manner by Scott and those close to him.

REASONS NOT TO RUN: Scott winning the Florida governorship presented a very steep—and very expensive—hill to climb. Millions of dollars of Scott's own fortune would have to be spent just to have a chance to win the Republican nomination. Even if he was willing to invest big bucks in the contest, winning would still be a long shot for a number of obvious reasons: 1) Scott was a relative newcomer to Florida with no roots in and little knowledge of the state and its history, people, and issues; 2) he was virtually unknown by Florida's millions of voters; 3) he had no experience, absolutely none, running for or serving in elective office; 4) he was not an effective public speaker and might be prone to blunders on the hustings; and finally 5) perhaps the most compelling reason not to enter the race, his opponents would gleefully tar him with the label "crook" and "con man" because of his inescapable connection with the shameful Columbia/HCA fraud case.

SCOTT'S GUT REASONS TO RUN: Sure, it would be tough to win both the Republican primary against McCollum and then beat the Democratic nominee, who he and others now assumed would be Alex Sink, a former top bank executive (Bank of America) and current chief financial officer (or CFO) of Florida, an elected position with cabinet status. Sink was also the wife of an illustrious attorney, Bill McBride, who had run for and lost the Florida governorship in 2002 to Jeb Bush, brother of the U.S. president. Scott sensed it would not be extraordinarily difficult to knock off McCollum who, despite being well-known to Florida voters and endorsed by practically every Republican bigwig in the state, came across as a shopworn politician with little charisma. Sink was another matter, at this point potentially a very tough candidate to run against, but if anyone could find a way to defeat her, Scott argued, it would be Rick Scott. So, among his gut reasons to get into the race were 1) Scott's enormous self-confidence and will to win, and 2) a weak primary opponent followed by an unpredictable contest against an impressive and apparently well-qualified Democrat, a woman Scott felt he might be able to beat when the time came, if it came.

MORE REASONS TO RUN: 3) Scott had plenty of money and no qualms about risking a big chunk of it to save the people of Florida and the nation from the menace of "Obamacare," which was not only "socialist" but "unconstitutional"; 4) he was a businessman, not a politician, who knew how to get things done, not a cautious, thumb-trilling, pie in the sky guy like your standard career officeholder; 5) he was, in his own words, "a pro-life and pro-family values Christian," a political stance he instinctively knew would go over well with most Floridians; 6) the U.S. and Florida economies were, in the parlance of the street, in the toilet at the time, plagued by abnormally high unemployment, a condition Scott could both exploit and pledge to work hard to rectify, a winning combination; 7) the country, including Florida, was experiencing a conservative resurgence with the Tea Party folks leading the way, and Scott knew that his message—more jobs, smaller government, less taxes and regulations on business and corporations, and no new taxes for anyone—would resonant with conservative voters; and 8) Scott had a friend in Texas, Rick Perry, the state's ebullient Republican governor, who could provide a quick tutorial on anything Scott needed to know about how to be a governor or governance in general.

After weighing the pros and cons, it was clear what Scott's decision would be, and in the end it was his and his alone. There was no holding back this industrious man, and on April 9, 2010, he officially announced his candidacy for governor of Florida. The calendar told him and his campaign manager, Susie Wiles, that the primary election, scheduled for August 24, was 85 days away; and if Scott was fortunate enough to win the Republican nomination by beating McCollum, the general election, set for November 2, was just 70 days after the primary. This meant that Scott would have 155 days, or less than six months, to convince Floridians to elect him their governor.

How does a candidate who is a complete cipher to the electorate get known well enough in 155 days to win the governorship of a state with a population of more than 19 million people? Yes, that's right: Television. He and Wiles, along with assistance from other key staffers, devised a simple, logical, subtly clever plan to saturate the state with TV and radio ads featuring Scott and his alluring campaign promises. To top it off, each ad would end with a dramatic *coup de théâtre,* in this case "Let's Get to Work!" The ingenious part of the plan was not only would it quickly introduce Scott and his platform to millions of Florida voters up and down the state in a completely positive setting, it also had the advantage of allowing him—a candidate with poor personal communication skills—to avoid much real-time contact with questioning voters and reporters. In fact, during the 155-day campaign, Scott adamantly refused to meet with newspaper editorial boards around the state, flouting a longstanding Florida political tradition.

Scott's entry into the race was greeted by the mainstream press with polite coverage and understated skepticism. Most insiders, including seasoned journalists who had covered numerous elections in the state, automatically decided Scott had little chance of upsetting Bill McCollum, who in April 2010 was far ahead in the polls for the Republican nomination. Most media, both print and electronic, played up Scott's current involvement with CPR and the effort to defeat Obamacare (coincidentally or not, the president's Patient Protection and Affordable Care Act had been signed into law on March 23, 2010, just a couple of weeks prior to Scott's entry into the gubernatorial race). A typical article carried the headline "Anti-Health Care Reform Crusader Rick Scott Enters FL-Gov Race" (*TPM* [talkingpointsmemo.com], April 13, 2010). The piece in *TPM* included salient passages from Scott's prepared statement, for example, "Florida needs a conservative who is not afraid to upset the apple cart, an outsider who is not part of the political establishment . . . and a businessman who knows how to create jobs, cut costs, balance budgets, and bring new ideas to old problems."

As far as Scott's tainted past was concerned, most political media decided to maintain a relatively neutral stance, opting to treat the Columbia/HCA fraud case as settled history that had minimal relevance in the Florida governor's race in 2010. But journalists knew it was a simmering issue that at anytime in the campaign could catch fire, a point driven home by the many negative reader responses to the Scott announcement reported in *TPM* and elsewhere. One reader wrote, "Perhaps a niggling point, but I've never understood why he [Scott] isn't in jail as well as having to repay the money ripped off from the federal government." Another wrote, "Medicare fraud. That'll go over big in Florida," and another, "The profit motive has replaced human decency as a core American value. This shyster should at least be off the public stage if not in jail," and another, "So does fraud qualify as a 'new idea' or an 'old problem'?"

But the pundits and citizens were dead wrong about Scott's prospects. As the campaign progressed, McCollum and Scott both engaged in some pro forma political mudslinging, but the Scott TV juggernaut proved too much for McCollum. As one reporter noted, "We can't hide from Rick Scott's commercials. They seem to compete with the regular programs for who gets the most airtime." Scott also had the most effective lines in the campaign, for instance promising he would create "700,000 new jobs in Florida in seven years." When later asked by a reporter if the 700,000 jobs were in addition to the one million new jobs economists projected would be added to the state's workforce over that time span due to growth alone, Scott readily asserted, yes, the 700,000 would be in addition to the projected number. Such a bold, confident candidate! To no one's surprise, "Let's Get to Work!" became the four most familiar words of the campaign. So, as the days before the primary peeled away, Scott the outsider—this odd looking man with the prominent bald dome and perfectly round eyes that never seemed to blink—continued to gain on McCollum and eventually overtook him in the polls. By midnight on primary day, August 24, 2010, Bill McCollum, who lost to Scott by 3 percentage points, had just finished giving his concession speech.

Rick Scott had little time to celebrate. He now faced a more daunting task. He had just 70 days to try to pull off another upset victory, this time against Alex Sink, an attractive, articulate, native-born Floridian who had high-level experience in the banking industry and was currently Florida's CFO. Again, Scott would start as the underdog.

3

Sidebar: More About The 2010 Florida Republican Primary

Each of these men—Mel Martinez, Charlie Crist, and Bill McCollum—is a Republican who in his own way contributed to the rise of Rick Scott as a significant player in the current political fortunes of Florida, the fourth largest state in the USA. Not long ago, each of these three men was a Florida politician with a bright future. Today, none holds public office, and odds are Martinez and McCollum, currently ages 66 and 68 respectively, never will again.

Charlie Crist, on the other hand, is different due to the fact that he is young enough (56 at this writing) to still have a future in elective politics—if he learns to read the tea leaves correctly. What happened to Charlie Crist after he announced in 2009 that he would give up Florida's governorship for a seat in the U.S. Senate is exactly the reverse of what happened to Rick Scott when he declared for governor. Scott's political career blossomed while Crist's wilted and currently is at risk of drying up and blowing away.

What exactly did Charlie Crist do that was so wrong? What caused his promising career to derail so quickly, and at some point might it be revived? What became clear in 2009-10 was that Crist's calculated decision to become a moderate Republican ultimately put him in bad odor with extremely conservative members of the GOP and especially the Tea Party, an emerging ideologically uncompromising rightwing political force in Florida as well as other states. Soon Charlie's high poll numbers began to slip, and eventually conservative Marco Rubio, a Tea Party favorite, not only began to pull away from Crist in the polls for the Republican senatorial nomination, but eventually forced the governor to quit the Republican primary and run for the U.S. Senate recast as an "unaffiliated" or independent candidate. Perhaps Crist's greatest sin in the eyes of the Tea Party was that well-publicized "man-hug" he gave President Obama in Fort

Myers back in early 2009. Rubio effectively used the hug, which became widely known as the "Hug of Death," to brand Crist a turncoat.

In the general election in November 2010, Rubio handily whipped both Kendrick Meek, the Democratic candidate, and the unaffiliated Crist. The question that remains is how seriously has Crist's political brand been damaged by his fall from Republican grace? It would seem at this time his ties to the Grand Old Party are irretrievably broken. But could it be that Crist might at some point find a new home and new vitality as a moderate Democrat, completing a transition from hard-right conservative to soft-left liberal? And might he choose to run for governor of Florida in 2014 as a Democrat?? Stranger things have happened in Florida politics. The state's politically savvy people, including Charlie Crist and Rick Scott, should keep the possibility in mind.

-4-

SCOTT ELECTED GOVERNOR OF FLORIDA IN CLOSE RACE

The headline "Rick Scott's Florida Republican Gubernatorial Nomination Leaves GOP Reeling" (voices: yahoo.com, August 25, 2010) summed up the general feeling of gloom among many Republican political leaders around the state upon learning that Scott would be the party's standard-bearer in the 2010 race for governor. Bill McCollum had been widely perceived to be the stronger candidate to take on Alex Sink, while Scott was looked upon as practically an alien, certainly an interloper. Sure, Scott had a lot of money, but he couldn't accuse Sink, as he had McCollum, of being a lackluster career politician. He couldn't simply because she wasn't. Moreover, Sink would doubtless hammer away at Scott's greatest vulnerability, his leadership of Columbia/HCA during all those years when the company was methodically defrauding the U.S government, a very legitimate issue that McCollum failed to exploit.

Still, the party couldn't disown its alien/interloper, and rather quickly establishment movers and shakers swallowed their disappointment and began to make nice with Scott, who, when they actually met and got to know him a bit, didn't seem to be all that awful. In fact, most people who encountered the man one-on-one found him to be mannerly and friendly, albeit more than a little stiff and ill at ease when it came to impromptu conversation and repartee. Miami reporter Michael Putney, who's been described as "the dean of South Florida television news," met Scott during the campaign and came away with this balanced assessment: "If you can penetrate his protective circle of advisors, Scott turns out to be good company. Pleasant, smiling and courteous. And yet he is extremely opaque and hard to read. He has his talking points and rarely goes off-message" (*The Reid Report*, July 29, 2010).

Also, Scott now had the backing of the state's two most influential business groups, Associated Industries of Florida and the Florida Chamber of Commerce. In addition, and this is most significant, by this time numerous voters had come to accept

Scott—or Scott's TV image—as someone they recognized. Some didn't like him and his ideas while others did. The point is, he was no longer looked upon by the majority of the electorate as some exotic creature who had just emerged in the Sunshine State from a black hole in deep space.

It's no surprise, then, that Scott's approach to running against Sink basically mirrored his campaign against McCollum, the key strategies being 1) lavish spending on television and radio commercials and assorted other means of getting him and his pro-business positions better known around the state; and 2) avoiding as much as possible live encounters with potentially inquisitive or hostile voters and journalists. Again, Floridians heard about the 700,000 jobs in seven years and the ubiquitous tag line "Let's get to work!" He also reiterated his promises to reduce the state's workforce, to make state employees contribute to their pension fund, to cut billions of dollars from Medicaid spending, to give the boot to all of those unnecessary state regulations that were stifling business and therefore job creation, to lower and eventual do away with corporate taxes, to lower property taxes, to crackdown Arizona-style on illegal immigration, etc. All of these needed changes would be accomplished, said Scott, while continuing full funding for education at all levels, something he had been told most Floridians favored. In a departure from the previous campaign, team Scott decided Alex Sink's political persona would have to be attacked much more aggressively than was McCollum's. In a word, Sink had to be "defined" whereas McCollum came to the race defined by his many years in government.

Most pundits considered the contest Alex Sink's to lose. After all, she had the resume, he had the scandal. But it soon became apparent that Sink was not an entirely effective political tactician or campaigner. Her voice frequently appeared to lack passion and a sense of urgency, and during the last week in August and the early weeks of September, she became almost invisible. While being bombarded by Scott's TV and radio ads, flyers, and the like, the pro-Sink forces began to worry, asking "Where's Alex?" Finally, her campaign began to gin up in anticipation of three crucial televised debates with Scott scheduled to take place in different Florida cities in October, all less than a month before the election. The first one was set for Friday, October 8, in Miami.

During this initial debate, the candidates, like boxers, cautiously probed for weaknesses in their opponent's style and delivery. Scott stuck largely to his now familiar lines, though he added a few new ones drawn from his commercials designed to muddy Sink's credentials. Among his well-rehearsed thrusts were, "She's an Obama liberal" and "She calls herself a fiscal watchdog [but] she won't take responsibility for anything." Patricia Mazzei, reporting on the debate in the *Miami Herald* (October 9, 2010), noted, "Sink went on the offensive more often than her opponent during the hourlong debate, an effort to blunt the effects of Scott's barrage of negative ads against her in the race." At this point, most polls had Sink slightly ahead, though the number of potential voters who viewed her negatively had now for the first time reached double digits.

The second debate, held in Fort Lauderdale on Wednesday, October 20, broke no meaningful new ground for either candidate. By this time the polls were showing a tightening of the race. The much anticipated third and final debate took place on Monday, October 25, in Tampa, just a week before election day. It was in this make-or-break debate a small off-camera incident occurred that by the next morning had exploded into damning headlines that possibly cost Alex Sink the election.

From the beginning, the Tampa debate was a raucous affair. It was the equivalent of the 15th round, and the candidates were now quite familiar with each other's favorite punches and parries. Each was looking to score a knockout. Ryan Mills, a reporter for the *Naples News,* posted his commentary online late that evening (naplesnews.com, October 25, 2010), in which he described the debate "as much an alley brawl as a prize fight . . . . The feisty—at times heated—bout may have helped turnoff voters who have witnessed the candidates throw jabs at one another for months during seemingly incessant television commercials." At one point Sink accused Scott of being a "corporate raider" and a "disgraced chief executive officer" who was lying about both his record and hers. Scott in turn accused Sink of planning to increase state government spending by $12.5 billion, and of being responsible for losing money in Florida's pension fund during her tenure as the state's CFO, charges Sink hotly denied.

But by far the biggest blow of the evening landed during a commercial time-out when Sink received a message on her cell phone from an overzealous campaign aide. Scott noticed this, which clearly was against the debate rules both candidates had agreed to, and in the words of a next-morning blogger, Scott "ratted her out on the air after the commercial break." The call gave the appearance that Sink and her team were trying to cheat. Later that evening Sink fired the aide, an attempt to show how strongly she condemned the call, but the damage was done. What made the innocuous call, which overnight became a huge blunder, even more detrimental to Sink's campaign was the timing. The incident had occurred so close to election day that Floridians who hadn't taken advantage of absentee or early voting would go to the polls with negative headlines about Sink, consciously or subconsciously, in mind.

Days earlier, the Sink camp had committed another mistake that was much more egregious than the cell phone call, but it never grabbed the attention of the voting public, most likely because it involved a legal issue that didn't lend itself readily to sound bites or castigating headlines. Briefly, in 2000 Scott had given a deposition in a civil case involving a dispute over a communications contract while he was still head of Columbia/HCA. In his deposition, Scott invoked the Fifth Amendment numerous times. This case had nothing to do with the federal government's criminal probe of Columbia/HCA, for which Scott had never been officially questioned or deposed. Yet Sink and her people launched a hard-hitting negative ad in mid-October implying that Scott had taken the Fifth 75 times when responding to questions concerning the criminal case. This, of course, was a blatantly false representation of the facts, something Sink and her advisers must have been aware of. But the unrelenting air wars between Scott and Sink toward the end of the campaign did not allow Scott's people time to deconstruct the ad and then prepare a stinging rebuttal the voting public could easily comprehend. As a result, Sink escaped widespread condemnation for this bit of campaign chicanery.

In the end, it's possible Alex Sink was sunk (pardon the irresistible pun) by what in retrospect was a minor mistake, a cell phone call from an aide during a debate break, while she got away with a serious ethical lapse by airing a commercial she must have known was based on a falsehood.

When all the votes were casted and counted on November 2, 2010, Rick Scott had won the race for governor of Florida by the relatively slim margin of 61,550 votes, or just over 1 percent of all votes received by the two principal candidates. Of the 5,359,735 total votes cast in the election, Scott received 2,619,335 (48.87%) and Sink 2,557,785 (47.72%).

It was the state's closest gubernatorial election in more than a century. And Scott was only the second Florida governor ever to win with less than 50 percent of the total vote.

Yes, Alex Sink had not run a sterling campaign, and perhaps snafus by her and her staff were responsible for the loss of a close election. But looking at the big picture, Scott's victory hinged on just one five-letter word: MONEY. There's no other way in the world a person with his disreputable background, his total lack of experience as a public servant, and his minimal knowledge of his prospective constituency, could possibly have become a viable candidate for—let alone elected to—the top executive position in a state as large and complex as Florida without bags and bags and bags of MONEY. It's difficult to nail down exactly how much Scott spent in his self-financed run for governor (most say it was more than $70 million; some say $80 million), but frankly the exact amount doesn't really matter, because it's well documented he outspent both McCollum and Sink by millions and millions of dollars. What it all comes down to is this: <u>Rick Scott bought and paid for the governorship of Florida just as he had once bought and paid for a chain of hospitals.</u>

After the election, it's quite possible more than a few thoughtful voters hoped and even prayed that Scott's new acquisition—the executive branch of Florida's government—would turn out much differently than had his scandalous venture into the world of hospitals and healthcare. Some, like this author, whispered, "Don't hold your breath."

Between November 2, 2010, when he was elected, and January 4, 2011, when he would be inaugurated, Scott and his transition team, headed by Enu Mainigi (pronounced Ee-new Ma-nee-gee), a Harvard-educated Washington D.C. attorney and longtime Scott confidante, worked to assemble an administration, a task that proved more complicated than had been anticipated. Some of the governor-elect's advisers were, like Mainigi and Scott himself, outsiders—people who did not have extensive or intuitive knowledge of Florida, a situation that created obvious problems. For instance, neither Scott nor Mainigi knew much about the specifics of the state's judiciary. To find out about the court system (e.g., which state judges were appointed and which

33

elected, and the length of their terms). Mainigi requested a memo detailing the "basics" from a staff researcher. Others on the transition team represented conservative special interest groups eager to capitalize on the new administration's extreme pro-business stance. Some of the ideas floated by these operatives bordered on the outlandish, e.g., mandating that Florida residents pay higher utility bills to subsidize cheaper rates for businesses as a reward for relocating in Florida. Other ideas were simply not feasible, e.g., mandating that people receiving unemployment benefits be forced to do community service work, a program set up for nonviolent criminal offenders to pay their debt to society. Or could it be that Scott and those around him considered unemployment a crime? With rare exceptions, the press had no access to the work of the transition term, Scott's watchword being "don't talk to members of the press."

Also during this time, Scott traveled the state, meeting business and political leaders as well as thanking voters for electing him. A highlight of his so-called "jobs tour" in December took him to Florida's Panhandle, the northwest region of the state known to Floridians as either the "Emerald Coast" or the "Redneck Riviera"—which term one uses usually identifies the person's political persuasion. Long a conservative Republican stronghold, the Panhandle voted for Scott in large numbers, and he was there to celebrate. In the city of Fort Walton Beach, for instance, a revved up governor-elect told a friendly crowd who turned out to cheer him, "This is our time. We're going to focus every day on building jobs. Jobs, jobs, jobs." An orator Scott is not.

Scott also used this time to put the arm on wealthy supporters to help finance his upcoming inauguration, envisioned as an expensive gala event to kick off his four-year term as Florida's big man in Tallahassee. He offered contributors VIP treatment at the event in exchange for a minimum donation of $25,000. Like magic, the state's largest corporations and developers coughed up 61 checks for the required amount. Some gave more, Blue Cross/Blue Shield contributing the most, roughly $500,000, a signal the health insurance company knew they had a committed for-profit man as Florida's new CEO.

In addition, between the period of getting elected and inaugurated, Scott received a lot of well-meaning advice, much of it prompted by the fact that he had no previous experience as an elected official. Some of the advice was solicited, some not. Among the former was from his good friend Texas governor Rick Perry, with whom he now talked on a regular basis via phone. Among the latter was ex-governor of Florida Jeb Bush (1999-2007), who provided more than two cents worth of advice to Scott in a gratuitous email. Jeb, the Republican governor who preceded Charlie Crist, is as most people know the brother of George W. Bush, a former president the United States, both of whom are sons of George H. W. Bush, also a former U.S. president. If Scott was intimated by the Bush brand or Jeb himself, a man who has an ego at least twice the size of as his substantial waistline, Scott didn't show it, as least publicly. Indeed, the governor-elect tended to ignore advice that didn't comport with his extremely conservative view of the world.

And naturally the media chimed in with all sorts of suggestions for the governor-elect. By way of example, an editorial entitled "A chance to clean up the capital" appeared in the *St. Petersburg Times* (November 4, 2010). It opined, possibly tongue-in-cheek, "Scott, who oversaw a hospital company that went on to pay record fines for Medicare fraud, may be an ironic tribune to the cause of cleaning up Tallahassee. But he has been elected governor, and it is up to him to set high standards for a more accountable government." That must have caused at least a few chuckles at the U.S. Justice Department. What's most interesting here is Scott's antagonistic relationship with Florida's newspaper press. He received not a single endorsement from a major newspaper in the state during either the McCollum or Sink campaigns, and he in turn made it a point more than once of letting the press and the public know that he did not read any widely circulated Florida newspapers.

Meanwhile, voters concerned with the state's future pondered what kind of governor Rick Scott might turn out to be. Despite being physically recognizable owing to all those seemingly endless TV commercials featuring him and his oft repeated political slogans plus appearances in the Sink-Scott debates, the soon-to-be governor remained an enigma to most Floridians. Pictures and words were one thing, deeds another. Some, such as Barry Bishop, president of Associated Industries of Florida, speaking for the state's business community, assured people that Scott is "a visionary executive who knows how to deliver . . . . that the thing we'll see is Scott's belief in Accountability with a 'capital A'" (*Florida Trend*, January 2011). Still, as Inauguration Day loomed, many other Floridians were uncertain about Rick Scott, sensing they might have bought a pig in a poke.

-5-

AMERICA'S MOST UNPOPULAR GOVERNOR

Tuesday, January 4, 2011, Inauguration Day in Tally (as denizens of Florida sometimes call their capital city) was bright and sunny, a good omen. A prayer breakfast held on the campus of Florida A&M University, the state's premiere black institution of higher learning, was the first item on the day's crowded calendar. The late Charles "Chuck" Colson, best known for his role in the Watergate scandal who after serving a prison sentence became an evangelical minister, provided the homily. Jennifer Carroll, Rick Scott's running mate and the first woman and first African American to be elected Florida's lieutenant governor, declared, "Rick and I, to the core, believe that God is our rock and foundation."

A few hours later, Scott, who turned 58 the previous month, stood on the steps of the state's historic Old Capitol building for the swearing-in ceremony, the oath administered by Florida Supreme Court Chief Justice Charles Canady. Then came the new governor's inaugural address, a 20-minute speech that was remarkable for its lack of new ideas and quotable lines. Scott repeated his commitment to reduce the state's alarmingly high rate of unemployment by focusing like a laser on job creation. In the same mode, he promised lean and limited government distinguished by lower taxes and reduced regulations on businesses, large and small. Scott also made it clear that privatization of various government functions would be a priority. Said he, "When government does the buying, when government chooses what services are available, the truth is, he pays the piper who calls the tune. Now we're going to call the tune, not government." A maladroit speaker prone to rushing and swallowing his words, Scott at one point made a Freudian slip, saying he would "get rid of some state agencies" when he meant to say "state programs."

Overall, Florida reporters, editorial writers, and media analysts were unimpressed by both the content and delivery of the speech, but most seemed prepared to grant the neophyte governor time to adjust to being a public servant accountable to the people as opposed to a captain of industry who rules by fiat.

The day's events also included a parade that passed in front of the Old Capitol featuring spirited performances by Florida A&M's celebrated Marching 100 band plus five high school bands from Collier County where Gov. Scott had lived until his move to Tallahassee. Later in the afternoon his new home, the Governor's Mansion at 700 North Adams Street, was opened to the public for a few hours. The busy day in Tallahassee concluded in the evening with the traditional inaugural ball, an observer noting it was "one of the most lavish inaugural parties in the country." Both city residents and visitors to the capital who came to witness the installation of Richard Lynn "Rick" Scott as Florida's 45th governor gave every appearance of being pleased with how well the occasion came off. Only a few protesters were spotted, the most conspicuous being a person holding a sign reading "Governor Voldemort," a reference to Lord Voldemort, a bald scoundrel in the Harry Potter gallery of rogues.

The new governor also found time to issue several executive orders (or EOs) on Inauguration Day. One imposed an immediate freeze on all rules and regulations about to be issued by state agencies under the governor's purview until such time as Scott and his staff could review each and every one, and there were hundreds. Another of Scott's EOs required state agencies to obtain the governor's approval for any contracts calling for expenditures of $1 million or more.

At the time, few Floridians had any inkling these orders were precursors of a torrent of controversial actions by Gov. Scott during his first months in office that would result in some of the lowest favorable opinion poll numbers ever recorded by an incoming Florida governor. Though he never promised to govern by consensus, Scott from day one was always on the lookout to grab and solidify as much power as he could, often using a sledgehammer approach to get what he wanted—behavior that inevitably offended large numbers of ordinary citizens as well as some state legislators and county and municipal officials. For instance, his first executive order irritated more than a few members of the Florida Legislature, who had already approved the rules and regulations Scott was about to scrutinize. Also, Scott's review, a time-consuming effort due to the large number of decrees involved, created delays and disruptions in the orderly flow of routine government business at both the state and local levels. The second order ruffled feathers too when his motive became clear: "It is no different than when I took over companies," bragged Scott. "One of the first things you have to do is get control of the checkbook." Soon the people of Florida would learn that MONEY, no matter what Scott concerned himself with, was not only the bottom line, it was frequently the only line.

In a signed opinion piece in the *St. Petersburg Times* (February 6, 2011), editorial writer Tim Nickens provided a succinct albeit devastatingly honest description of Scott's attitude toward his role as governor: "Barely a month has passed since Gov. Rick Scott took office, and it is clear he views his new job as Florida's chief executive no differently than his old job as chief executive assembling the nation's largest hospital chain. *It's just another hostile takeover"* (emphasis added).

Soon people began saying some very unkind things about the new governor, calling him "an embarrassment," "clueless," "one of the most entertainingly shameless figures in American political life," "the prince of darkness," "the worst governor Florida's ever had," "PinkSlip Rick," "Rick the Prick," and other names best not repeated here in a book intended for the whole family.

Soon protesters were regularly showing up to heckle Gov. Scott whenever he left the mansion. In March, for instance, he was the featured speaker at a Florida Republican Party event at the New World Landing in Pensacola. More than 150 teachers and union members gathered outside, picketing and voicing their unhappiness with Scott. Even some GOP stalwarts inside the banquet hall expressed dissatisfaction with his handling of the job. One attendee criticized the governor for not explaining his policies clearly: "Anytime you change things, you have to articulate a plan, and some of his [Scott's] plans and programs haven't been well articulated." In early April he came to St. Petersburg on Florida's Gulf Coast to throw out the first pitch at Tropicana Field where the Tampa Bay Rays were about to begin their 2011 major league baseball season. Using Facebook, a protest group signed up roughly 1,200 people to come to the park to "Boo Rick Scott on Opening Day," which they did vociferously. Later that month organizers of the annual "Springtime Tallahassee" festival invited the new governor to be the grand marshall of its parade. Put charitably, Gov. Scott received less than an enthusiastic reception, especially from fired state workers distinguished by their "PinkSlip Rick" placards.

Also in early April, hundreds of Florida voters signed a petition posted online calling for Scott's impeachment. In the words of the petition, "It is time to investigate and impeach this self-promoting man. Florida can do better!" The petition, however, stood no chance of ridding the state of its unloved governor. Only the state's House of Representatives has the power to impeach a Florida governor, and the House in 2011 was dominated by right-wing Republicans who for the most part supported Scott's initiatives. It should also be noted the Florida Constitution makes no provision for recalling elected state officials, unlike, for instance, what recently occurred in Wisconsin in connection with that state's polemical governor, Scott Walker.

At this point Gov. Rick Scott's poll numbers vacillated between dismal and disastrous. By the end of his first month in office, a Quinnipiac University poll indicated only 28 percent of voters viewed Scott's job performance as favorable. In March, Public Policy Polling reported 32 percent of Floridians approved his handling of the job while 55 percent disapproved; the same poll found that in a hypothetical repeat of the November 2010 gubernatorial election, Alex Sink would now beat Scott, 56 to 37 percent. In May, the Quinnipiac poll showed Scott's favorable rating had risen to 29 percent. Almost every poll showing how Floridians viewed the job Scott was doing as governor from early January to the end of June had him stuck at either just under or just over 30 percent approval.

What follows are samplings of Scott's policies and actions that earned him the unenviable reputation as "America's Most Unpopular Governor" during his first six or so months in office. (Note: Additional information about the issues discussed below can be found in Appendix 1. "Notes on Gov. Scott's Handling of the Major Issues, January 2011-April 2012"; see pages 61-105.)

*From the beginning Scott showed contempt for Florida's venerable Sunshine Law that mandates public officials conduct the public's business in the open, not secretly behind closed doors. The law also stipulates broad public access to records generated by state government. An example of Scott's hostility toward open government involved email records. As both governor-elect and governor, he instructed his staff and department heads to avoid using email when conducting state business. Why? Because such messages are public documents and therefore should in most cases be available to the public, which in the world of Rick Scott is tantamount to revealing trade secrets. And on those occasions when top level personnel in the Scott administration did use email to communicate, the messages were quickly deleted, a violation of Florida law. Scott, of course, insisted none of this was done on purpose. Each time it was an honest mistake, or someone hit the wrong button, or the dog ate the emails. The Florida Department of Law Enforcement eventually investigated missing transition records, finding that Scott's campaign manager Susie Wiles "closed down the email accounts without consulting the governor and without realizing data would be lost" (Associated Press report, June 21, 2012). Shades of Columbia/HCA practices . . . .

*When Scott came into office, the U.S. Department of Transportation (DOT) had an offer of $2.4 billion on the table for Florida to launch a national high-speed rail system, the first leg of which would connect Tampa and Orlando. This unique opportunity for Florida would not only create thousands of good paying jobs in a state suffering from high unemployment, but in time, like the Interstate Highway system before it, high-speed rail service would be a boon to economic development in every section of the state. Moreover, the Florida Legislature had already approved the deal. But Scott, the so-called "jobs governor," took it upon himself—unilaterally—to reject DOT's offer. Despite bipartisan pleas to accept it, and iron-clad assurances the state would not be held responsible for any cost overruns or deficits caused by overly optimistic ridership projections, Scott arrogantly said no, no, no, and no again. As one of the many editorials denouncing the new governor's decision observed, "Logic and bipartisan support are no match for a stubborn ideologue." And obviously Scott's burning animosity toward President Obama played a role in the decision.

*Scott's visceral dislike of Obama and his policies was also evident when he and the Florida Legislature refused millions of dollars allocated by the federal government to prepare for the implementation of the Patient Protection and Affordable Care Act, the complex new national healthcare law passed by the U.S. Congress and approved by the president in March 2010. Scott later shocked just about everyone when he tried to justify his harebrained decision to reject the money by claiming the new act is "not the law of the land." The U.S. Supreme Court held hearing on the constitutionality of the healthcare law at the end of March 2012, with a final ruling expected a few months later, probably in June. But Scott decided he couldn't or wouldn't wait for the high court to render its judgment. In one of his most insolent pronouncements, he himself ruled the law "not the law."

*Scott's first budget (fiscal year 2011-12) called for cuts of $1.3 billion in spending for education, a blatant disregard of his campaign promise to maintain education funding at 2010-11 levels. People wondered how the "jobs governor" would attract businesses to relocate in Florida when the state's spending on education was among the lowest in the nation—and he had just lowered it yet another notch or two.

*Speaking of budgets, Scott chose to sign his first budget in May 2011 at The Villages, a mega retirement community straddling three Florida counties (Lake, Sumter, and Marion). The biggest urban complex in North Central Florida, the sprawling Villages currently has a population of almost 95,000 residents, the overwhelming majority of whom are conservative Republican and Tea Party types and, as might be expected, pro-Scott supporters. Normally, budget signing ceremonies in Florida are low-key events held in Tallahassee, but Scott, apparently weary of catcalls and jeers everywhere he went, decided to make the 2011 signing at The Villages more like a campaign stop with friendly crowds and upbeat speeches extolling what a wonderful fellow he is. Then, horror of horrors, a dozen elderly Democrats, all Villagers, showed up holding small anti-Scott signs. A man with a name tag indicating he was a member of the governor's entourage quickly appeared, ordering the offending Democrats removed, which ultimately was accomplished by a Sumter County sheriff's deputy. According to one of the protesters, they were told the governor was "trying to create an image, and we didn't fit in." This illegal treatment of a few people trying to exercise their First Amendment rights prompted, to put it bluntly, a terrible stink all over the state, encouraging many Floridians to question the new governor's grasp of the United States Bill of Rights. Scott later denied knowing anything about the incident, which has become his stock answer to all embarrassing questions. But he did pledge to look into the matter, wink, wink.

*Environmentalists were another group Gov. Scott alienated early on by proposing to defund Florida Forever, a highly successful program wherein the state buys and preserves large tracts of Florida's undeveloped land. In the past, Florida Forever had been supported by both Democratic and Republican governors. In another anti-environmental move, Scott advocated dismantling the state's Department of Community Affairs, which administrated Florida's 1985 growth management law, a progressive piece of legislation intended to reign in rapacious developers and their tendency to create unchecked sprawl in urban areas. Former Florida Gov. Bob Graham, who made it a point not to criticize those who followed him into the office he had held for two terms in the 1980s, finally grew so frustrated with Scott that he publicly spoke out, chastising the new governor for his myopic perspective concerning Florida's fragile environment.

Unfortunately, Graham's efforts had no impact on Scott, who knew very little if anything about the state's geologic and hydrologic makeup or concerns. In June 2011 Scott signed off on a bill that did away with the Department of Community Affairs, replacing it with a new agency, the Department of Economic Opportunity (perhaps better named the "Department in Charge of Selling Florida's Natural Resources"), and new legislation that gutted good growth management principles. Graham and pro-environmental groups also lost the battle in 2011 to fund Florida Forever.

Yet another troublesome issue for Gov. Scott—his manic desire to privatize any and all government functions—added a host of new voices to the chorus of discontent with his extreme pro-business policies. The people of Florida were quickly learning their new governor intensely dislikes the public sector. They were learning that he's a "for-profit" man who finds public accountability and transparency foreign concepts; that he believes if an enterprise doesn't make money, it's not worth anyone's time. Hence his irresponsible rejection of Florida's opportunity to initiate a national public high-speed rail system; hence his unjustified refusal to prepare for the implementation of a new federal healthcare law that will benefit millions of people in the state he governs; hence his efforts to privatize parts of the state's public parks system, the state's public school system, the state's public prison system. You name it and Scott will or has tried to privatize it.

As might be expected, from the beginning Gov. Scott did not go out of his way to befriend rank-and-file state employees. In fact he, along with many of his most ardent conservative boosters, tended to view workers in the public sector as overpaid and underworked, often describing them in derogatory terms, such as "lazy bureaucrats" and "parasites." Scott, who managed to lay off at least 3,500 people who worked for the state for in 2011 (with more than 4,000 slated to get the ax in 2012), did his best to help foster these stereotypes by issuing an executive order soon after becoming governor that would require most state employees to be tested periodically for illegal drug use. The American Civil Liberties Union of Florida challenged Scott's action with a lawsuit, but before it could be adjudicated the 2012 Florida Legislature passed a law giving the governor statutory authority to drug-test employees. That legislation, fortunately, has been found to be unconstitutional.

*In 2011 Scott, again with the eager complicity of the Legislature, attempted to cut the take-home pay of public sector workers in Florida by signing legislation forcing them to contribute a portion of their salary to the state's pension fund, called the Florida Retirement System (FRS). Heretofore employee contributions to FRS, which covers municipal and county as well as state workers, had been paid in-full by the agencies they work for, a benefit granted by contractual agreement negotiated with the state of Florida in 1974. In March 2012 the new law was invalidated by a Leon County circuit judge. The Scott administration appealed that decision to the Florida Supreme Court where it is currently being considered.

*The legal actions involving public employees and FRS mentioned above were just a few of numerous lawsuits naming Gov. Scott as a defendant during his early months in office. The suits, which often resulted from the governor's failure to recognize the constitutional limits of his power, have already cost taxpayers many millions of dollars to litigate, and some are still not yet settled. Lawsuit issues other than those already described run the gamut from public school teachers' bargaining rights to student-led prayer at public school functions to the right of physicians to discuss gun ownership with patients. If nothing else, Scott has generated lots of work for the Florida legal profession.

To sum up, Rick Scott's first six months as Florida's governor were something of a disaster for everyone except corporatists, the very rich, and the business and legal communities. And even they could count on only short-term gains from a man who appeared hellbent on denigrating all that was good about Florida. Gov. Scott gave little indication of sensing the chaos he was creating around the state, or if he did, he appeared to enjoy it. Like a large psychopathic child full of enormous energy but no awareness of social norms, he dabbled here, there, and seemingly everywhere, looking to punish those who disagreed with him and reward those who did. He came across as a person practically devoid of introspection and compassion, a man who cared for nothing if you couldn't put a monetary value on.

In short, most Floridians and Scott himself came out of the ordeal of the early months much worse than anyone could have imagined on that sunny Inauguration Day in early January when he raised his right hand to take the oath of office on the steps of the Old Capitol. From the beginning, Scott tried to run the state as if it were a for-profit enterprise, a mistake that took him down a path that resulted in his becoming the nation's most disliked governor. After watching this faux "public servant" for half a year thrash around weakening and diminishing the state of Florida, some citizens, including this writer, came to the sad conclusion that Rick Scott was never fit to be the state's governor and during his initial months in office he proved it convincingly.

Paula Dockery, a maverick Republican member of the 2011-12 Florida Senate from Lakeland, best described the essence of Scott's problems with the electorate: "He's governing very far to the right and that's alienating everyone who's not very far to the right" (Associated Press report, July 14, 2011).

Scott, on the other hand, professed not to be bothered by the low poll numbers, the protests, the impeachment petition, the many lawsuits, the general disparagement of his ability to govern openly, honestly, fairly, and reasonably. He put a gloss on it all by saying he was doing the tough things that needed doing, and he didn't expect to be wildly popular or the object of adoration.

Almost defiantly in early July 2011, more than three years before the event, he announced he would run for reelection in November 2014. Apparently Scott did not want disgruntled voters getting the wrong idea that he might become depressed or frustrated enough to quit after only four years of buying and selling Florida. No, like that bad smelling stuff that sometimes sticks to your shoe, he would hang around for as long as he could. And he would, he believed, find a way to be reelected. Think $$$ . . . .

-6-

RICK'S IMAGE MAKEOVER

Despite Gov. Scott's protestations to the contrary, he did care very much about how he was—and is—perceived by voters, peers, and the media. For instance, his widely reported assertion that he refused to read Florida newspapers turned out to be untrue. "He has always read news stories," reported Brian Burgess, the governor's communications director. "He stays very well informed." So it was in the spring of 2011, after experiencing poll numbers that would make a Cheshire cat cry, Scott started contemplating ways to improve his image. Soon he and his aides concocted several amateurish public relations gimmicks designed to turn the most unpopular governor in America into someone a majority of Floridians might learn to like or, at the very least, tolerate.

The first and most successful of these PR efforts, launched in April, put Scott behind a microphone at mostly small, low-power Florida radio stations where he would spend half an hour or so making friendly chitchat with conservative talk show hosts who were more than willing to lob him softball questions about his goals as governor, his childhood, his family, his favorite things to eat—listeners at one station, for example, learned the governor especially enjoys lobster bisque and smoked salmon. Controversial issues were normally verboten, though he welcomed the opportunity to talk in generalities with his hosts or callers about his marquee policies, i.e., creating more jobs for Floridians, lowering the unemployment rate, reducing taxes on businesses, and downsizing state government. While precious little news emanated from these appearances, occasionally a Scott gaffe would get reported, as when he claimed Florida was the only state in 2011 to cut taxes. Between April and July, the always exceedingly hard-working Scott did some 130 of these radio gigs. All indications are his handlers believed the governor was benefitting politically by using local radio shows to project a positive persona to constituents.

Another early Scott PR ploy turned out to be much less successful and died a quick death. Someone in his inner circle—perhaps Scott himself—came up the idea of composing a form letter praising the governor as both a dynamic leader and a caring man. The self-serving document, posted on his website, rickscottforflorida.com, reeled off a number of the governor's alleged achievements during his first few months in office, while also ballyhooing his superior personal qualities, which included enormous courage exhibited in the face of unwarranted attacks by liberal special interest groups that were unrelenting in their efforts to disparage this dedicated man and his tough-love policies. Scott was also described as "refreshing" and deserving of the people's "unwavering and enthusiastic support." Supporters were urged to copy all or parts of this bit of puffery and send it to Florida newspapers, the intent being it would appear in many papers around the state as a letter to the editor. Soon Floridians who were critical of their new governor would learn that he had many devoted followers from Pensacola to the Florida Keys, from Jacksonville to Naples, from Palm Beach to St. Pete Beach. But Scott's smarmy campaign to elicit praise came a cropper when political columnists and editorial writers responded by ridiculing the letter as a pathetic attempt at self-promotion. The ridicule went national when TV funny man Stephen Colbert got ahold of the story. Using his best deadpan delivery, Colbert suggested Scott would "probably be doing better [in the opinion polls] if he wasn't trying to kill Harry Potter," a reference to the evil Scott lookalike, Lord Voldemort, whose bald pate Colbert juxtaposed on screen with Scott's.

Yet another effort to improve Scott's standing with Floridians involved self-congratulatory canned telephone calls to voters. Everyone is familiar with such calls, known as robocalls, during election campaigns, but Scott decided to use the tactic after the election was over as a means of getting out the word regarding his sterling accomplishments. Again, instead of earning the tin-eared governor higher approval numbers, the robocalls antagonized a great many citizens, including Republicans, who publicly voiced their disgust by complaining on radio call-in shows, in letters to news publications, and by calling or emailing the governor's office directly. One irate voter put it this way: "We are all used to getting robocalls during campaign season, but to continue to get them AFTER the election is unprecedented and extremely disturbing! . . . . Funny how a guy that preaches limiting government intrusion in our private lives is DOING JUST THAT with this harassing robo-phone campaign." Unfortunately, Floridians annoyed by Scott's unwelcome calls found that being on federal or state Do Not Call lists did nothing to alleviate the problem, as political calls are exempt from such lists.

Obviously, as the summer of 2011 approached, things weren't going well with the country's most unloved governor. Not a stupid man, Scott realized he needed expert help with his image building project. Poll numbers had hardly moved at all and, if they had, the direction was downward. In fact, the form letter and the robocalls most likely did more harm than good, and the radio appearances seemed to do little more than shore up his conservative base. What he needed, he decided, was a substantial shakeup involving key members of his administration. This tall, bald, awkward, controversial man, who had tirelessly clawed his way up from the depths of the lower middle class to become a successful attorney and then a superrich businessman and now head honcho of America's fourth largest state, sensed he needed new blood, a new approach, one that would eventually achieve his goal of acceptance by a broad segment of the people of Florida and eventually help secure his reelection. As a result, in June he made several high-level staff changes, the most significant being the hiring of a new chief of staff: Stephen Raymond "Steve" MacNamara was a battle-tested operative described by those who closely follow Florida political intrigue as "a quintessential Tallahassee insider."

Rick Scott, the quintessential Tallahassee outsider, believed Steve MacNamara just might be the right person to see him through a period of major change. Not a change involving core political beliefs, no sir, no way. But rather a change that would radically remake his facade, his public persona, his image.

There's no doubt that Gov. Scott welcomed the day in early July when the 58-year-old MacNamara (who was just a few month younger than Scott) started work as his new chief of staff. A man with a resumé in government service as impressive as his new boss's was deficient. Steve MacNamara held a degree in journalism from the University of Florida and a law degree from Florida State University. Most recently, he had been Florida Senate President Mike Haridopolos's chief of staff, and earlier he served in the same position with former Florida House Speaker John Thrasher, thus giving MacNamara the distinction of being the only person to serve as chief of staff for leaders of both houses of the Florida Legislature as well as the state's governor. In the 1970s he worked as campaign manager for two well-known Florida politicians, Democrat Bruce Smathers and Republican Claude Kirk, and at the beginning of his career he interned with Dempsey Barron, long one of the most powerful—and feared—Florida legislators in the postwar era. In addition, MacNamara was a tenured professor at Florida State University, teaching in the Communications Department since 1984. He had also worked at two of the state's major law firms as well as the nonpartisan Collins Center for Public Policy. On top of all this, MacNamara had considerable experience as one of the most enduring functionaries in the world of politics: lobbyist.

The word around Tallahassee was Steve MacNamara never slept, or if he did, it's with one eye open. It's also said he couldn't abide small talk, disliked being touched or even to shake hands, could be charming but when annoyed had a fiery temper. Moreover, he believed in strictly following an established chain of command, which in his new job placed him on the rung just below the governor. Capital insiders wondered how well the greenhorn governor and the extensively experienced new chief of staff would work together? For a while everything seemed to go swimmingly.

One of MacNamara's first moves as the governor's righthand man was to cancel an interview Scott had scheduled with Michael Putney, a prominent television reporter for Miami's ABC affiliate, WPLG, and host of the Sunday program "This Week in South Florida With Michael Putney." Putney, who made the mistake of sending his questions to Scott prior to sitting down with him, published his account of the

Interview That Never Was in a column in the *Miami Herald* (July 12, 2011). "Maybe I was a bit too direct in my questions," wrote the stiffed reporter. "On Tuesday, the governor's chief of staff, Steve MacNamara, canceled the interview, calling some of my questions 'insulting.' Too bad; there was no insult intended, just tough questions during tough times."

Putney then went on to spell out half a dozen questions he had prepared to ask Scott: 1) "Are you clueless when it comes to accepting money from Washington? You turned down $2.4 billion for that high-speed rail line from Tampa to Orlando and $19 million more to lay the groundwork in Florida for health care reform." 2) "Medicaid is not only useful, it's essential for millions of low-income Floridians. True, it's taking an unsustainable chunk of the state budget, but is turning health care for the poor over to for-profit private insurance companies the answer?" 3) "Why do you think that in almost every sphere of endeavor the private sector is better than government?" 4) "What were you thinking when you signed the new state budget at a ceremony sponsored and staged by the Republican Party of Florida [at The Villagers] where only tea partiers and other true believers where let in and nonbelievers were kicked out?" 5) "When you vetoed more than $600 million from the state budget you said you were getting rid of 'frivolous and wasteful spending.' Nobody's for that, but a lot of folks think tax money is well spent on Farm Share which gives away donated produce and other food to thousands of needy people across the state. You cut $750,000 from Farm Share. And how about the $500,000 nixed from the Dan Marino Foundation, which helps autistic and other developmentally challenged kids?" 6) "An outfit from Malaysia that runs big casinos and resorts just plunked down $236 million for the *Miami Herald* property and wants to build, among other things, a casino . . . . Do you support destination casinos?"

These would have been tough questions for the carefully scripted Scott to handle, especially when pressed by an experienced adversarial interviewer like Putney, who doubtless would have insisted on real answers, not just talking points. Was it Scott or MacNamara who made the decision to beg off the Putney interview? That's an unknown at this point, but more than likely MacNamara recognized the danger and advised Scott, who didn't protest, to authorize cancellation of the Q&A with Putney.

A month or so later the new chief of staff again established his bona fides with Scott when MacNamara clashed with the governor's recently hired secretary of Florida's Department of Corrections. Previously head of Indiana's prison system, Edwin Buss had been heavily recruited and richly rewarded by Scott based on his reputation as a cost-cutting, reform-minded prison administrator. However, Buss's tendency to make decisions and public statements without first clearing them with the governor or MacNamara led to an eyeball-to-eyeball power struggle. Especially galling to Scott was Buss's public support for a lawsuit filed by Florida's corrections officers' union over the hot issue of privatizing a large number of the state's prisons. Not only was Scott the moving force behind the privatization effort, but the union had vigorously opposed his election as governor. Ultimately, after a bruising closed-door meeting, Ed Buss was forced to resign, having served only seven months in the job. Interestingly, just hours <u>before</u> Buss got the heave-ho, Scott and MacNamara offered the position to a man who, though he had considerable law enforcement experience, by his own admission had no real knowledge of how to run a prison system. Fine, said the governor and his chief of staff: You're just the man we want!

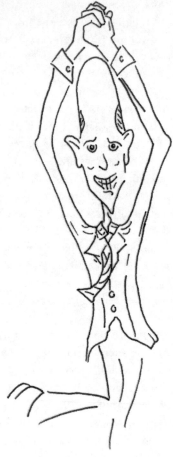

"End Corporate Taxes"

Of course, MacNamara's main task in the summer of 2011 entailed devising a plan to give Rick Scott a new public face, one that would humanize him, and might in time transform the out-of-favor governor into a politician Floridians would come to view as a capable, trustworthy leader. Given what MacNamara had to work with, this was not an easy assignment. Just considering Scott's poor public speaking skills made any image makeover problematic. But the new chief of staff was used to challenges, and he knew ideally what politicians need to do to be successful. And the job was made easier because the governor, who knew he had to do something to reverse his negative image before it hardened in the public mind, was eager to cooperate with any logical plan MacNamara proposed. The biggest concern? Was Rick Scott—a secretive, tightly wound, self-centered, linguistically unprepossessing, often bullheaded human being—really capable of making the necessary adjustments required to substantially change his public image?

The first step in Gov. Scott's makeover was a snap. MacNamara decreed the governor had to quit wearing his ubiquitous dark suits, dress shirts, and paisley ties that he had favored as business attire, swapping them instead for a more sporty look, including button-down shirts, no ties, and khaki trousers. As befitting his status, Scott's new shirts included his name, the word "governor," and the Florida state seal above the breast pocket. MacNamara apparently agreed Scott might continue wearing his beloved cowboy boots, a habit he developed while living in Texas. Like his shirts, Scott's boots, which are custom-made in Houston and cost a bundle, displayed the Florida seal along with the words "45th Governor." Not long after taking office, Scott told a reporter, "I'm a boot guy. That's all I wear. Not when I go the beach though. I'll wear sandals. Or I go barefoot because it feels good." Sartorially, Scott now projected a downright casual image.

The second facade change involved "workdays," wherein Scott would spend a day about once a month actually working at a particular job somewhere in the state. Such highly photogenic outings were designed to show the governor rubbing shoulders with everyday Floridians in a variety of settings, hopefully resulting in good press for all concerned. Former Gov. Bob Graham, credited with introducing the workday concept in 1974 while a state senator, continued using it with great success during his eight years as governor (1979-87). Scott added a couple of winkles of his own, announcing his workdays were to be known as "Let's Get to Work Days" and would consist mostly of jobs he had once performed in humbler times. As he told *Florida Trend* in an interview with the magazine's editors in the March 2011 issue, "I didn't start out with great jobs. I worked as an 85-cent-an-hour fry cook, I delivered papers for a penny a paper, I cleaned telephone booths, I worked at amusement parks, I cleaned latrines . . . ."

Gov. Scott's first Let's Get to Work Day took place in early August at a doughnut shop in Tampa that harked back to his earlier doughnut days in Kansas City. Always animated by any endeavor that involved making money, Scott appeared to enjoy working behind the counter, interacting with customers and frequently proclaiming, "Our job is sell out all these doughnuts" and "We need lots of people to buy these doughnuts." Some respectful protesters showed up at the well-publicized event; when one of them placed an order, Scott said, "I'm glad you're buying doughnuts." Actually, the store sold every doughnut it had that day—more than 80 dozen. The governor, however, got burned later when, in his televised second annual State of the State address (January 10, 2012), he told the audience the shop had sold "more than 240 dozen doughnuts by 8:30 a.m." none of which was true. Some might dismiss this as a silly little error, while others (like this writer) might conclude if Scott can't get the doughnut count anywhere close to being correct in a major speech, how can you trust anything he says?

Other Scott workdays have included preparing and serving breakfast and lunch at an elementary school in Orlando, teaching a couple of classes on American government at Immokalee High School where the children of migrant laborers sometimes go to school, helping out at a restaurant in Panama City Beach, assisting homeless people at a Tallahassee soup kitchen, working at a naval base, and spending a day at the Port of Miami entertaining passengers about to embark on a cruise ship headed for the Bahamas. Thus far, the workday stratagem, which presumably will continue for the rest of Scott's term, appears to be a modest success, with Scott getting a certain amount of positive press. Like the radio gigs, he professes to enjoy meeting and talking with just plain Floridians.

The last major component of MacNamara's program to remake the fledgling governor's image and turn around those atrocious poll numbers proved to be the most difficult for Scott to achieve, and is still a work in progress. It concerns repairing his badly strained relations with the Florida press—a relationship that got off to a disagreeable start right at the beginning of the Republican primary campaign in 2010 when he frequently shunned reporters and flatly refused to meet with the editorial boards of Florida's leading newspapers. Indeed, Scott gave the general impression that members of the press were enemies of the state.

Things didn't get any better during the transition period or early months of his governorship, when Scott imposed all sorts of restrictions on access to information, including public records. Although Florida's Government-in-the-Sunshine Law dictates that most state, county, and municipal records "are open for personal inspection and copying by *any person*," Scott's staff was usually in no hurry to process requests for state documents. In addition, the governor began adding substantial fees to handle such requests. For example, Scott's newly imposed fee schedule cost a Florida blogger $784.84 for <u>one week</u> of email records between Scott and his communications director, whereas the state of Alaska recently charged less than that to produce <u>two years</u> worth of all Sarah Palin's emails when she was the state's governor. Scott, for whom money has almost always been the first and foremost priority in any transaction, actually told a group of journalists that he was more concerned about the cost of staff time spent retrieving public records than he was in carrying out the legal mandate to make them readily available. "Part of my job," said the gauche governor, attempting to justify the fees, "is to make sure I don't waste taxpayer money," implying processing requests for public records is a waste of time.

Gov. Scott also enjoyed letting the press know who was boss. In a telling exposé published in the February 3, 2011 edition of the *St. Petersburg Times* (now *Tampa Bay Times*), Lucy Morgan, the paper's senior correspondent, described how, at an event held at the Governor's Mansion that included a number of Florida legislators, Scott used his power to manipulate and humiliate the Capitol Press Corps. Florida's public meetings law allows reporters to be present at such events, but Scott insisted only one reporter would be permitted to attend—and he would choose that reporter, which was not the way it had been done previously when more considerate governors were in office. According to Morgan, "The governor summoned Nancy Smith, editor of a Web news site called Sunshine State News, an organization that will not disclose the identity of its owners. Some have suggested the governor himself may have an interest in it." Several days after the event Smith published a column that did little more than describe the governor as 'utterly charming' and a 'hero,' which naturally, to put it colloquially, pissed off a lot of seasoned Florida reporters.

MacNamara must have told Scott that if he didn't change his attitude toward open government and the central role of the press in that process, he would almost certainly be a one-term governor, and Scott apparently got the message. So, though it wasn't the easiest thing in the world for him to do, the governor launched a charm offensive intended to improve his standing with Florida's fourth estate.

From the time he began to campaign for the governorship, Scott received daily morning briefings by staff members concerning the day ahead. In July 2011, soon after MacNamara's arrival, a half-hour was added to the schedule for a "media briefing," designed to alert Scott to current concerns of the state's reporters and editors. Then on Monday, August 1, almost seven months after he had been sworn in as governor, Scott met for the first time with the Capitol Press Corps in his Tallahassee office. At that gathering he revealed his intention to begin meeting with newspaper editorial boards. He also dropped the word that one of his upcoming Let's Get to Work Days might take place at a Florida newspaper, where perhaps he could lend a hand in the circulation office—after all, he had experience as a youngster delivering newspapers. Continuing his efforts to butter up the press, a week later Scott held an extended Q&A session with journalists. At one point, the governor gushed, "You know, I always wanted to buy a newspaper. I even looked to buy a newspaper." For good measure, he added "I like newspapers, and I like the paper newspaper."

Scott kept his commitment to meet with editorial boards, first sitting down with the *Tallahassee Democrat*, and then the *Miami Herald*, the *South Florida Sun-Sentinel*, the *Tampa Bay Times*, the *Tampa Tribune*, the *Orlando Sentinel* and so on. Word leaked out, however, that not all of these meeting went smoothly, especially when the governor was evasive or refused to go beyond his prepared script. Unlike the radio shows and workdays where he came into contact with ordinary people whom he can easily manage or brush off, editorial board members were as a rule very well informed and articulate professionals who wanted substantive answers concerning the political questions of the day. In fact, Scott appeared to be quite uncomfortable at times during some of these meetings, and for good reason: He could not help but sense board members often had much greater knowledge and depth of understanding of the state of Florida and its concerns than did he, a relative newcomer. As Mark Howard, executive editor of *Florida Trend*, put it in an editorial in the January 2012 issue of the magazine, Gov. Scott "just isn't on a first-name basis with the state in the same way as more experienced veterans of the state's political and business scene . . . . Scott's lack of first-hand experience—wisdom earned from actual experience with issues and the people in Florida—has, I believe, contributed to his ideological rigor getting in the way of both his and the state's success."

In a nutshell, efforts to co-opt or win over the hearts and minds of members of Florida's press corps were the most demanding—and so far least successful—aspect of Rick Scott's image makeover.

So, by the end of April 2012, when the governor had completed 16 months, or one-third, of his four-year term, how had the MacNamara formula for improving Scott's image panned out? Had the image-changing regimen moved his poll numbers into favorable territory? Put another way, had Gov. Scott and his policies become more palatable to the people of Florida? *Florida Trend* (March 2011) reported the governor "enjoys fawning support from business groups," and that observation continued to be true more than a year later. No doubt about it, early in his administration Scott had established himself as arguably the most pro-business, for-profit governor in the history of Florida, and corporate interests rewarded him with near total fealty.

But what about the millions of Floridians who, though they of course wanted enough financial security to have a decent life, measured success by more than money alone? What about the people who valued such "assets" as clean water, quality public schools and universities, high quality medical care, fair and inclusive elections, humane treatment of the elderly and the poor, effective public transportation, intelligent management of the state's explosive growth, sensible regulation of firearms, preservation of the state's award-winning public parks system, and elected officials who do not shrink from combating public corruption that documented sources indicate is rampant in Florida?

These "assets" and others like them, which normally cannot be measured by the single metric of money, are high priorities for many Floridians. It's no wonder, then, that Scott's governing philosophy of giving practically everything to corporatists and leaving a few crumbs for everyone else is unacceptable to a majority of voters. Did Scott, MacNamara, and company really believe that if the governor changed his clothes from stuffy to casual and stroked a few egos on workdays and in the press that no one would notice that his administration, with the help of hard-right conservative cohorts in the Florida Legislature, was neglecting, diminishing, or destroying such public resources as unpolluted water and sensible growth management policies? Did Scott and those in the bubble with him really think millions of Florida's citizens wouldn't mind that public education, public healthcare, public parks, public transportation, public safety, etc. had all suffered negative consequences during the governor's first 16 months in office? Or that during those months ordinary citizens wouldn't care that he and the Legislature schemed to lower or eliminate taxes on businesses at the expense of individual taxpayers, and to reduce commonsense regulations that protect the public from a multitude of corporate sins?

Indeed, the governor's new casual duds, smiley workdays, and calculated efforts to accommodate the press and embrace the concept of government in the sunshine appeared so far to have had little effect on Scott's poll numbers. Yes, he had the business community firmly on his side, along with his natural base—staunch Republican conservatives and the Tea Party claque. But the governor was not winning over those millions of Democrats, moderate Republicans, and independents who found his right-wing political agenda ideologically inflexible and lacking in humanity. Major opinion polls during the period July 2011-April 2012 gave Scott an approval rating averaging around 35 percent. As one commentator put it, the poll numbers have "ticked up to the point where he [Scott] is now merely loathed by Florida voters, rather than despised." In September, a whiny Gov. Scott told a group of Republicans in Orlando, "I've paid a price in popularity for sticking by my principles," adding that he was the victim of "liberal special interests that support government bailouts." What a laughable statement. In December, Public Policy Polling reported his approval number had hit a new low—26 percent. PPP noted, "What's really caused the bottom to drop out for him [Scott] is that even Republicans are starting to really sour on his leadership . . . . Scott [remains] the most unpopular governor in the country."

But, as often happens in the volatile opinion polling business, the next month a poll conducted by Mason-Dixon Polling & Research reported his favorability rating had shot up to 43 percent, indicating that, hey, maybe MacNamara's prescription is working after all. On the other hand, another poll around the same time found that only 12 percent of Florida Republican voters said Scott's endorsement of one of their party's presidential candidates would make them more likely to support that candidate, while 41 percent said less likely. With numbers like that, the presidential candidates ran away from Scott—fast as they could. In the last poll taken just before April 2012, the usually trustworthy Quinnipiac survey showed 36 percent of Floridians approving the job he was doing with 52 percent disapproving. And, just as this book was going to press in May, a poll of registered voters by Florida Opinion Research indicated that former Gov. Charlie Crist, running for governor in 2014 as a Democrat, would beat Rick Scott by 48.1 to 34.1 percent (with 12.8 percent undecided and 5 percent for other candidates).

Further signs of Gov. Scott's lack of popularity with his constituents were signaled by the way Democrats constantly and joyfully lambasted him every chance they got, as if he were a big piñata ripe for the beating. For instance, in June 2011 leaders of the Florida Democratic Party, who gathered in Broward County for their annual Jefferson-Jackson fundraising event, mocked Scott as "our number one supporter. What would we do without him?" Later, in September, vice president of the U.S., Joe Biden, speaking in Orlando at the party's 2011 convention, blasted Scott for cutting funding for education, for advocating an Arizona-style immigration law, and for rejecting more than $2 billion to initiate a national high-speed rail system. Also at the convention, Bob Butterworth, a much respected former Florida attorney general, characterized Scott as "an embarrassment to our state." In October, Democrats launched Rickpublicans.com, a fundraising website that identified Republican muckety-mucks said to be chummy with Scott, the idea being that his lack of popularity might shame or scare off a few of the power brokers who were supporting him. The site began by defining "Rickpublican" as a noun: *"Proper name for Florida Republicans wrought with greed and corruption who are hell-bent on selling out to the corporations and special interests while leaving Florida's middle-class families out-to-dry."*

Another reason the polls continued to indicate dissatisfaction with Scott's handling of his responsibilities as governor include the fact that, though he adopted the mantle of Florida's "Jobs Governor," having promised 700,000 new jobs in seven years during the campaign, in reality he hadn't delivered many jobs in his first 16 months. He was quick to take credit for every new job created, most of which he had little or nothing to do with, but he maintained a tight-lipped silent when the numbers turned negative, as they did in November 2011 when approximately 1,100 jobs were lost in the state, and again in January 2012 when there was a huge jobs deficit of nearly 39,000, and yet again in April when 2,700 more jobs were lost. In the area of job creation, Scott came across, as they say in Texas, as "all hat and no cattle." (See Appendix 1, pages 86-93, under JOBS, JOB CREATION, AND UNEMPLOYMENT for a more detailed look at Scott's sorry record on jobs.)

Also, poor public speaking skills and verbal blunders continued to plague Scott, often making him look foolish or incompetent. In an informal assessment of the governor's freshman year aired December 30, 2011 on Tampa's WUSF-PBS TV program "Florida This Week," Rosemary Goudreau, former editorial page editor of the *Tampa Tribune,* noted that Scott "keeps stepping in it." Case in point: When in October 2011 Scott finally revealed his grand plan for creating jobs (ten months after he had assumed office!), he made a pitch for increasing the number of university students majoring in Science, Technology, Engineering, and Mathematics, the so-called STEM subjects. He emphasized that STEM is where the best paying jobs are or will be, adding ungrammatically, "How many more jobs you think there is for anthropology in this state? You want to use your tax dollars to educate more people that can't get jobs in anthropology? I don't." Of course, the remark created a firestorm of criticism directed toward the blissfully shallow governor by anthropologists and other educated people who appreciate anthropology and other social sciences as important academic disciplines, especially in a state like Florida that has a rich cultural history dating back to pre-Columbian times, something Scott obviously knows little about. An interesting sidebar to this episode: One of Scott's daughters has a degree in anthropology.

Another negative that helped keep Scott's poll numbers in the dumpster was his tendency to tell Floridians one thing and do the opposite, a ploy used so often that many savvy voters stopped listening to him. By way of example, he was frequently quoted as saying how much he cares about Florida's environment: "We want to take care of our environment. You look at places in Florida and how well they developed—look at Naples—you see that they did a great job. You really have to admire it." He's on record as saying similar things about the Everglades. Yet when it came time to make up his budget proposals and suggest funding—adequately funding—for environmental projects, Scott is almost always on the other side of the ledger. What he has done to gut the state's water management districts ranks as a scandal in the making, a story that has yet to be fully comprehended or told. (See Appendix 1, pages 72-74, under ENVIRONMENT AND ENERGY—MANAGEMENT OF FLORIDA'S WATER for more about this issue.)

But the most compelling reason Scott remains unpopular with and viscerally disliked by so many Floridians is his unyielding pursuit of a radical pro-business agenda that mimics the wacko right-wing ideology espoused by ultraconservative organizations such as Americans for Prosperity, a foundation headed by the billionaire Koch brothers, David and Charles. In late June 2011, the governor sneaked off to Colorado to attend a hush-hush retreat hosted by the secretive brothers. Later, after a sharp-eyed reporter discovered the governor had been at the gathering, which included his old buddy Texas Governor Rick Perry, he was asked why he went there and what he had learned? "In this job [meaning being Florida's governor], you've got to constantly listen to what other people are thinking. Part of what you do in business is you say, 'Gosh, they are doing something, well, I'm going to see if I can do it better'." But in Scott-land, listening to new ideas applies only if conservatives like the Koch brothers are doing the talking. He's on record as stating, "I'm not going to appoint people that don't believe what I believe in."

A glaring example of this attitude occurred when Scott relied on a report by the right-wing Reason Foundation when deciding to reject more than $2 billion in federal money to start building a high-speed rail system in Florida. A more recent instance was his absurd decision to authorize Florida Polytechnic in Lakeland as the 12th member of the state's university system. Currently the state is unable to adequately support eleven universities let alone twelve. And it's not as if Florida Polytechnic is some thriving school that has long waited for the right to be independent. No, at the present time the "university" has no buildings to speak of, no faculty, no students, and no prospects of accreditation for years. Scott, however, decided to forge ahead—irrationally—and fund the so-called university, apparently to satisfy the wishes of one overbearing conservative Florida state senator.

Back to the original question: Did Steve MacNamara's prescription to improve Scott's image boost his standing with Florida voters? The answer: Hardly at all, at least in the short run. Has it enhanced the governor's chances for reelection way off in November 2014? Maybe, but at this point it's too soon to tell. Still, MacNamara did achieve something quite remarkable. He apparently convinced Rick Scott—called by some the Prince of Darkness—to change his public attitude toward the press and accept the need for a certain amount of transparency in the governing process. In fact, just as Scott was concluding his first 16 months as governor, he introduced a new policy inspired by MacNamara designed to provide public access to the many hundreds of emails that flow daily to and from the governor's office and eleven of his highest ranking staff members. Called Project Sunburst, this new effort at bringing openness to the business of Florida's government won Scott praise from his critics in the press. Steve Bousquet, Tallahassee bureau chief for the *Tampa Bay Times* put it this way in the paper's May 22, 2012 edition: "The candidate who refused to meet with editorial boards in 2010 now does so often. The governor-elect whose emails were carelessly deleted during his transition to power now lets the public see email online. That's progress." Of course time will tell if Scott lives up to the promise of Sunbburst.

Project Sunburst was Steve MacNamara's last effort to help Gov. Scott achieve a new, more palatable public persona. Eventually MacNamara wore out his welcome in the Scott administration. He had quickly accrued an enormous amount of power as the governor's chief of staff, which included being Scott's gate-keeper. Some of Scott's cronies began calling MacNamara "Florida's shadow governor," complaining the hard-nosed aide was shutting them out of the inner circle, which indeed had shrunk considerably during MacNamara's tenure. Also MacNamara had stealthily been feathering the nests of some his close friends, giving them plum jobs in state government or steering no-bid contracts their way. Eventually the press uncovered and revealed some of these dealings. Marc Caputo, writing in the *Miami Herald* (May 6, 2012), dug into MacNamara's past, finding him "ethically challenged," pointing out, "Questions about MacNamara's integrity go back a decade. In between his stints as staff chief to the Florida House Speaker [John Thrasher] in 1999 and 2000, MacNamara secretly worked out a lobbying gig to help persuade the state to reverse course and permit a cement plant on the scenic Ichetucknee River." After a spate of similar articles, Scott and his top staffer sat down for a private meeting and when they emerged MacNamara had resigned, leaving the administration in July, a year after he had come onboard.

The MacNamara plan to change Scott's image tends to reinforce the general conviction among political analysts that superficial contrivances rarely change voters' minds about a politician. Not always, but usually, voters are swayed by a candidates perceived stand on the issues, and not how they dress or engage with the proverbial man on the street or deal with the press. At the end of 16 months of his 48-month term as Florida's governor, Rick Scott's poll numbers remained dangerously low for someone with reelection on his mind. Why so low? In essence it all goes back to Paula Dockery's shrewd observation: "He's governing very far to the right, and that's alienating everyone who's not very far to the right."

-7-

A Citizen's J'accuse: Rick Scott Unfit To Be Governor Of Florida

At this point there's not much left to be said about Richard Lynn "Rick" Scott, the attorney-cum-hospital czar-cum-venture capitalist-cum-Florida governor. The preceding six chapters, plus the lengthy appendix that follows, tell the story of a man driven to overreach at every turn. It's an oft-told American tale of a compulsively driven person who grew up in economically stressed circumstances whose only values as an adult are expressed in monetary terms. Regrettably, such a person often lacks tolerance, compassion, and intellectual curiosity, plus that overworked word, vision.

This doesn't mean Rick Scott is not a complex human being. In fact in a creepy sort of way, he's commendable. Most people who had been the hands-on president and CEO of a huge business enterprise for ten years that was found guilty and heavily punished for systematically defrauding the federal government of massive amounts of taxpayer money, would have retreated into private life, too contrite or ashamed to venture outside the cocoon provided by family and a few loyal friends and colleagues. Scott took the exact opposite tack, and that took guts—or maybe the conscience of a psychopath?

In any event, few people would give a fig about Rick Scott and his ill-gotten millions if he hadn't bought the governorship of one of America's largest and most iconic states. The overriding questions are: 1) Has Scott so far been an evenhanded, flexible, effective governor? and 2) Would Florida benefit by having nearly seven more years of him as governor, should he be reelected in November 2014?

Anyone who has read this book up to this point can easily predict my answer to both questions: Rick Scott never was fit to be Florida's governor, nor is he fit now or ever to be its governor.

You can disagree if you want. But I challenge you to make a convincing case.

It's regrettable Gov. Scott cannot be recalled or impeached. The former is not possible because the Florida Constitution lacks a provision for the recall of a governor, and the latter is most unlikely because the Florida Legislature, where impeachment and conviction would occur, is currently dominated by politicians much like Scott himself.

Those of us who find Scott's extremist policies and programs abhorrent basically have two options. First, we can continue to vigorously oppose this unfit governor day-by-day, week-by-week, month-by-month, year-by-year; and second, we can work, work, work, work, and work some more to defeat him in November 2014. Think of it: In his first 16 months as governor, Scott has done enormous harm—some of it irreparable—to the state we live in and love. It's almost impossible to contemplate the damage he will do in the next 32 months. And the idea of 48 more months of Scott as governor after that is simply unfathomable.

An admonition: Do NOT fall for any of Scott's superficial image makeovers or smiling political commercials. There's no doubt he will employ more and more gimmicks to appear competent and likable, and will saturate television, radio, and the Internet with commercials showing himself as a friendly, avuncular figure who wouldn't harm a little beach mouse. Always remember, he's governing hard-right.

I'll continue my "Scott Watch" between now and 2014, when I plan to update this little book prior to the gubernatorial election in November of that year.

Ken Kister

APPENDIX 1

NOTES ON GOV. SCOTT'S HANDLING OF THE MAJOR ISSUES, JANUARY 2011-APRIL 2012

This section of the book provides summaries of Gov. Scott's positions and actions on key issues he dealt with in his first 16 months as Florida's governor.

As readers are aware, most of these issues are referenced briefly (or at least mentioned) in the body of the book, usually to illustrate some aspect of Scott's political philosophy or approach to governing. The purpose of Appendix 1 is not to rehash what has already been said; rather, the idea is to offer a systematic overview of the major issues and how Scott responded to them.

DRUGS AND DRUG TESTING

The key issues: 1) An epidemic abuse by Floridians of powerful painkilling prescription drugs; 2) Random testing of two groups of citizens—state employees and welfare recipients—for illegal drug use; and 3) Legislation to provide treatment for drug addicted prison inmates.

PRESCRIPTION DRUGS: Florida was—and still is—the so-called "pill mill capital of the nation," accounting recently for about seven deaths everyday in the state. For a number of years, efforts to control the problem centered on establishing a state-run prescription drug monitoring program via a database intended to identify pill abusers who go from physician to physician, and pharmacy to pharmacy, to obtain such potentially lethal painkilling opiates as oxycodone and Xanax. Such a database would also help identify doctors who overprescribe this class of drugs. Finally in 2009, after years of trying, a monitoring system was approved by the Legislature and then Gov. Charlie Crist. However, soon after becoming Florida's governor, Rick Scott sought to kill the program by defunding it in his first budget. He justified his decision by citing cost (<u>always</u> his first reason for doing the wrong thing) along with patient privacy concerns. Eventually he reversed course in the face of an outpouring of protests from his own attorney general (Pam Bondi), several powerful legislators, many concerned physicians, most law enforcement officers, and practically all grieving parents who had lost children to the epidemic. Latest reports indicate the monitoring database, which at last became operational in September 2011, is starting to make a difference, though the pill-mill problem in Florida is far from being eradicated.

DRUG TESTING: Gov. Scott has made it abundantly clear by his actions that he does not especially care for either of the two groups affected, i.e., state employees and welfare recipients. A short time after taking office in 2011, he issued an executive order (EO) requiring rank-and-file state workers to be randomly screened for illegal drug use. On the same day a bill was filed in the Florida Legislature calling for similar screening of Floridians who receive cash welfare assistance from the state, including the unemployed. All tolled, upwards to 200,000 Floridians could be subjected to testing.

Not surprisingly, law suits quickly materialized opposing both the EO and the proposed legislation, which later was adopted by the Legislature and signed into law by Scott. In the fall of 2011, ruling on a suit brought by the American Civil Liberties Union of Florida, a federal judge in Orlando granted a temporary injunction against testing welfare recipients. Scott is currently appealing that decision. Then in 2012, the Legislature passed a bill, which Scott quickly signed, giving the governor statutory power to drug-test state workers. Objections to drug testing both groups hinged on an obvious constitutional question: Is it permissible for the state to force law abiding citizens to undergo "suspicionless" drug tests simply because they work for state government or receive cash benefits from the state—benefits to which they are legally entitled? Legal precedence strongly suggests that where no probable cause exists, such tests constitute a form of invasion of privacy and a violation of the Fourth Amendment of the U.S. Constitution, which prohibits "unreasonable searches and seizures" by the state . . . . BREAKING NEWS: Just as this book was being readied for publication, U.S. District Judge Ursala Ungaro in Miami ruled that Gov. Scott's order requiring drug testing of state workers is unconstitutional. As with the case involving welfare recipients, Scott has indicated Judge Ungaro's decision will be appealed.

Indeed, Gov. Scott seems determined to continue to pursue his love affair with suspicionless drug testing, a policy he falsely claims "the public and Florida's taxpayers overwhelmingly support" (Associated Press report, April 26, 2012). All the while, he and his cabinet and members of the Florida Legislature are exempt from the procedure. A case can be made that the governor's unspoken goal is to intimidate and humiliate people he doesn't like or respect.

TREATMENT FOR DRUG-ADDICTED PRISON INMATES: In 2012, after trying for six years, state Sen. Ellyn Bogdanoff finally got the Florida Legislature to pass a bill allowing nonviolent state prisoners addicted to drugs to receive rehabilitation treatment while serving their sentences. Regrettably, Gov. Scott vetoed the experimental program, which had strong bipartisan support. He implied the legislation represents going soft on crime and, furthermore, promulgation of the bill might lead to some inmates serving less than the mandatory time (85 percent) required by Florida law for felons. A disappointed Sen. Bogdanoff was quoted as saying, "We'll try again."

EDUCATION

There's no doubt present-day Floridians want the best possible education for themselves and their children. In 1998, the Florida Constitution's Article IX, Section 1, which deals with public education, was amended to begin with these words: "The education of children is a fundamental value of the people of the state of Florida. It is, therefore, a paramount duty of the state to make adequate provision for the education of all children residing within its borders. Adequate provision shall be made by law for a uniform, efficient, safe, secure, and high quality system of free public schools that allows students to obtain a high quality education and for the establishment, maintenance, and operation of institutions of higher learning and other public programs that the needs of people may require."

Sad to say the state's political leaders, past and present, have not come close to fulfilling the promise of these lofty words. In so many criteria that measure the quality of education in the U.S., Florida ranks near the bottom.

The key issues: 1) Funding for education from K-12 to public colleges and universities; 2) The role of charter schools in the K-12 system; 3) Teacher dissatisfaction with changes concerning their status in the K-12 public school system; 4) Student-led prayer in public schools; 5) The STEM initiative; and 6) The new Florida Polytechnic University in Lakeland.

FUNDING FOR EDUCATION: In his first budget (2011-12), Gov. Scott cut $1.3 billion for K-12—this after promising during the campaign not to cut funding levels for education. The $1.3 billion represented a spending cut of approximately $600 per student per year. In his second budget (2012-13), the governor claimed to see the light and made a big deal about adding $1 billion to the budget for K-12. Said Scott in a promotional piece circulated for reprinting in local community newspapers around the state, "A good education is essential to getting a good job, so I have proposed adding $1 billion for K-12 education. This is the third largest amount of state funding for K-12 in the past decade." The governor forgot the say that the year before he short-changed K-12 by $1.3 billion. He also forgot to mention that Florida had added roughly 30,000 more K-12 students since his last budget, meaning his so-called "increase" was just another of Scott's familiar shell games.

In addition, in both his first and second budgets Scott endorsed cuts totaling hundreds of million of dollars for the state's public universities and colleges. In fact, 2012-13 was the fifth budgetary year in row higher education in Florida had been forced to absorb substantial cuts. Pam Iorio, former mayor of Tampa, wrote in an article entitled "A Lesson in Bad Leadership" in the *Tampa Bay Times* (February 16, 2012), "Why do we continue to make severe reductions to our state university system when we should be investing in higher education?" The discouraging answer is Scott and the right-wingers who currently control the Legislature believe it's more important to reduce or eliminate corporate taxes than to devote dollars to education. This is hardly the way to achieve a world-class educational system, said to be one of Scott's supposed goals; when unenlightened politicians intrude in things academic, don't count on logic being high on the agenda.

CHARTER SCHOOLS: As is well known by this time, Gov. Scott is a rah-rah champion of privatizing practically every government function. It's hardly surprising, then, that he, along with former Republican governor Jeb Bush, is at the forefront of the charter school movement in Florida, which currently steers millions of tax dollars from public schools to privately operated "academies" that have little public oversight and fail more often than not. For example, in the state's 2011-12 budget, Scott allotted exactly zero dollars for construction and maintenance of Florida's 3,355 public schools, whereas he managed to find $55 million for the state's 459 charter schools. In similar fashion, the governor supported much tougher standards for how public schools are currently graded, the sub rosa motive being that when a public school fails, a new charter school might take its place. Indeed, in the 2012 session of the Legislature, charter school proponents lobbied hard to pass a proposal called the "Parent Empowerment Act" (also known as the "parent trigger" bill) that would have allowed parents of children attending a failing public school to demand changes, including converting it to a charter school. The effort was defeated by a close bipartisan vote in the Florida Senate, but obviously the issue will return in a future session, most likely sooner than later.

PUBLIC SCHOOL TEACHER DISSATISFACTION: In September 2011, the state's largest teachers' union, the Florida Education Association (FEA), filed suit on behalf of several teachers concerning a new state law (actually, the first piece of legislation Gov. Scott signed) that redefined how Florida's 180,000 public school teachers would be paid, evaluated, hired, and fired. The FEA brief charged that some of the provisions of the statute violated teachers' collective bargaining rights—rights previously granted by the state. For instance, the contested law tied teachers' pay to student performance on standardized tests (such as the controversial Florida Comprehensive Assessment Test, or FCAT), and required school boards to fire teachers with the lowest evaluations, no matter their seniority, if staff cutbacks should become necessary. As of April 2012, the FEA suit is still being litigated.

Scott also vigorously supported legislation that mimicked efforts in some other states (e.g., Ohio; Wisconsin) to weaken or break teachers' unions. In Florida the proposal, which ultimately failed, would have disallowed automatic payroll deduction for union dues.

Professor Diane Ravitch, a prominent educator and author of *The Death and Life of the Great American School System: How Testing and Choice are Undermining Education* (Basic Books, 2010), served as keynote speaker at the Florida School Boards Association's spring conference in 2011. In her address, she blasted Scott's education policies: "Gov. Rick Scott seems determined to ruin public education in Florida. Not only is he devastating school budgets . . . but he is intent on crushing the morale of the state's teachers. One can't expect to improve public schools while demeaning the professionals who work in them . . . . Florida is on the cusp of a dangerous transition, one that will not prepare its children to be the thinkers, inventors, and entrepreneurs of the 21st century. On the contrary, Florida is developing a school system that will prepare young people for the repetitive factory jobs that left our shores long ago. And Florida will be a state that self-respecting teachers leave or shun."

PRAYER IN PUBLIC SCHOOLS: In its 2012 session, the Legislature passed a law that permits student-led prayer in public schools. Obviously the product of election-year catering to the worst instincts of ultraconservative Floridians, this boneheaded legislation will surely be challenged in the courts and ultimately found unconstitutional when adjudicated. Of course, Gov. Scott, who appears to have rarely met a bad idea he can't support, signed the bill "quietly and without fanfare."

THE STEM INITIATIVE: In mid-October 2011, ten months after assuming the governorship of Florida, Rick Scott finally unveiled the cornerstone of his "Let's Get to Work" jobs program, which can be summed up in one acronym: STEM. That is, if more students in Florida were to study Science, Technology, Engineering, and Mathematics, they will eventually, according to Scott, be rewarded by a plethora of high-paying jobs. Forget about studying literature, history, the fine and performing arts, foreign languages, philosophy, the social sciences, etc. And especially anthropology. In Scott-land, majoring in such subjects will surely land former students on the unemployment rolls along with all the other "parasites."

Don't believe it.

Although the governor spent a few weeks ballyhooing STEM, the idea seemed to quickly fade from public consciousness, especially when people realized he wasn't willing to put any serious money behind the idea. Instead, he implied schools, colleges, and universities should direct a larger share of the diminished tax money they currently receive toward STEM students while cutting back on those majoring in what might be called the "less desirable" subjects. This can only be described as a thoughtless notion floated by, frankly, an ignorant person. Later, presidents of Florida's two most prestigious state universities, the University of Florida (UF) and Florida State University (FSU), lobbied the governor for special permission to raise tuition rates at their schools, the extra money going to support a beefed up STEM curriculum. Again, this is not the way to build a world-class university system, STEM or no STEM.

After the initial hoopla concerning STEM began to die down, questions started to be asked about the wisdom of trying to get in on the ground floor of a concept that is half a century old and has already been exploited for years by other states. Writing in *Florida Trend* (October 2011) in an article appropriately titled "Hold Your Horses, Rick," Cynthia Barnett pointed out, ". . . when it comes to universities as generators of private companies and high-paying jobs, Texas has a big head start. The University of Texas at Austin has been spinning off and recruiting major technology companies since the late 1950s and early '60s, when Gainesville [home of UF] and Tallahassee [home of FSU] were still sleepy college towns." A similar observation can be made about North Carolina, whose Research Triangle comprising Duke University, North Carolina State University, and the University of North Carolina at Chapel Hill, has been open for business since 1959.

The fact that Scott's STEM initiative appears to be remembered more for his negative comments about anthropology——"You want to use your tax dollars to educate more people that can't get jobs in anthropology? I don't"——than for how the study of science, technology, engineering, and math will lead students to an abundance of lucrative jobs says a lot about Scott's inability to articulate and promote a complex jobs program. It's also interesting that a few months after unveiling STEM, the "jobs" governor cut the budget for higher education in Florida by $300 million.

FLORIDA POLYTECHNIC UNIVERSITY: In 2012 the Legislature approved Florida Polytechnic as the state's 12th and newest public university; only Gov. Scott's signature was required to complete the deal. Located in Lakeland, Florida Poly, as its commonly being called, has (or will have) a STEM-heavy curriculum, but currently the school also has a few nagging drawbacks, such as no campus, no faculty, no students, no accreditation. The pet project of controversial state Sen. JD Alexander, then chair of the Florida Senate Budget Committee, Florida Poly began its existence as part of the University of South Florida (USF), whose main campus in Tampa is a short drive via I-4 from Lakeland. Sen. Alexander used every ounce of his muscle as lord of the budget to bully fellow legislators into detaching the polytechnic school from USF and rechristening it a new university.

After this startling development, the looming question became what will Gov. Scott do about the legislation creating Florida Poly? Will he approve or veto it? It was quite clear that, given Scott's extremist pro-business tax policies, Florida could not adequately support eleven state universities, and certainly not twelve. And the nettlesome Sen. Alexander, about to be term-limited out of the Legislature, would no longer be around after 2012 to make trouble. On the other hand, Florida Poly could eventually, years and many, many millions of tax dollars down the road, help produce some STEM-related jobs. Just as this book was being readied for publication, Gov. Scott, in his convoluted wisdom, approved Florida Polytechnic as the state's newest university. In a press release, the governor suggested the new school with its focus on STEM will "generate positive return on investment," adding that "the new university will not result in additional financial strain on the State University System." Sure, we believe you, "Shell-Game" Rick.

After all this drama, most reasonable Floridians were again left to ponder who is responsible for this totally absurd way of going about growing and maintaining a state university system that, at best, currently could aspire to a grade of no more than C-?

To summarize: Rick Scott, the state's 45th governor, did nothing during his first third of his four-year term in office to move the state closer to achieving the constitutionally mandated goal of "high quality" education for all Floridians. In fact, Scott's ignorance of the state's educational needs, and his mania for privatizing K-12 schools while cutting funding for public schools and the state's institutions of higher learning, have led to increased uncertainty for students, teachers, professors, administrators, parents, and tax payers.

ELECTIONS AND VOTING RIGHTS

In the years 2011-12 Americans were inevitably more concerned than usual with politics due to the quadrennial exercise of choosing a president. It also seemed inevitable that Florida's highly partisan new governor, Rick Scott, could not help but become involved in some manner or other in the electoral process. Thus it was that early in his administration Gov. Scott found himself on the wrong side of three actions that reek of voter suppression.

The three issues: 1) A bill approved by the Republican-controlled legislature and signed into law by Scott that was promoted as legislation intended to put a stop to widespread voter fraud in Florida. But because there were few documented cases of voter fraud in the state in recent years, the real intent of the law was exposed as a calculated effort to discourage certain groups who normally vote Democratic from going to the polls; 2) A contentious effort by the Scott administration to purge potentially ineligible voters from the election rolls; and 3) The practice of delaying restoration of felons' civil rights, which include the right to vote, for years after they had served their time in prison. Because a disproportionate number of felons are black, this too was widely viewed as a reprehensible means of suppressing potential Democratic votes.

VOTER FRAUD LAW: The so-called "anti-voter fraud law" followed a national Republican strategy to change election rules to favor their party in the upcoming November 2012 elections in battleground states, which included Florida. The Florida election law appeared to many to have been crafted deliberately to suppress votes by such Democratic-leaning groups as African Americas, Hispanics, college students, senior citizens, and poor people. Specifically, the law reduced the number of early voting days from 14 to eight; eliminated early voting on the Sunday before election day (which was aimed primarily at black voters, many of whom traditionally go to the polls after attending church on the Sunday prior to the election); required those voters (e.g., college students) who want to change their voting precinct on election day to use a "provisional" ballot, which often did not get counted; and placed onerous restrictions on third-party groups that register new voters, such as the League of Woman Voters and the Washington D.C. group Rock the Vote. The law requires that those signing up new voters must register with the state and that new voter application forms must be submitted within 48 hours. The penalty for failure to register can be up to $1,000 and $50 for each late application form. Regrettably, the venerable League of Women Voters (LWV) suspended its nonpartisan voter registration activities in Florida rather than risk being fined—not due to doing anything wrong but because the new rules were considered unreasonable.

The new law not only curtailed traditional election activities of the LWV but generated horror stories involving individuals. A case in point: New Smyrna Beach High School teacher Jill Cicciarelli preregistered fifty 17-year-old students to vote at the beginning of the school year in 2011. This innocent exercise in American democracy went awry because, as a third party recruiting new voters, Cicciarelli had not registered with the state nor had she submitted the new voter application forms within the 48-hour deadline. (The teacher had been on maturity leave earlier in the year when the law went into effect, and she had not heard about the new rules.) As a result, Cicciarelli faced fines for her role as an unauthorized voter registration agent and for each late application form. One editorial writer observed, "That's some expensive civics lesson." Other teachers also got caught in the bureaucratic barbed wire of Florida's new election law. Anyone interested in a similar case can check out Santa Rosa County teacher Dawn Quarles, using your favorite search engine.

Like so many of the issues Gov. Scott became entangled in during his first 16 months in office, the new election law became the object of a legal challenge that is still pending. Three organizations—the LWV, Rock the Vote, and the Florida Public Interest Research Group Education Fund—brought a lawsuit against the Scott administration contending the registration requirements in the law are too restrictive in 62 of Florida's 67 counties. Note: Because of a past history of discrimination against minority voters, five Florida counties—Collier, Hardee, Hendry, Hillsborough, and Monroe—require "preclearance" (or pre-approval) from the U.S. Justice Department before any changes in state law pertaining to voting can go into effect in those five counties. The Justice Department has this authority under a provision of the landmark 1965 Voting Rights Act. In typical arrogant fashion, Gov. Scott, who had recently signed a state law that discriminates against minorities, ordered his chief elections officer, Florida's secretary of state, to petition a federal three-judge panel to lift the preclearance requirement from the five counties, suggesting federal oversight is no longer necessary. Just as the new law itself remains in litigation as of April 2012, so too the panel of judges had yet to rule on the Scott administration's preclearance request.

PURGE OF VOTER ROLLS: Working from some hopelessly flawed lists, the Scott administration first claimed there could be as many as 180,000 noncitizens on the state's voter rolls, out of a total of more than 12 million voters. (Note: Anyone not a U.S. citizen who votes commits a third-degree felony.) The list of 180,000, which was heavy on ethnic names, eventually got reduced to approximately 20,000 and then whittled down to 2,700, and even that list proved to be inaccurate and outdated. A *New York Times* article (June 9, 2012) quoted Vicki Davis, president of the Florida State Association of Supervisors of Elections, as pointing out, "Too many voters on the state's list turned out to actually be citizens." At this point, the U.S. Justice Department ordered Gov. Scott to halt his effort to purge the Florida rolls, but Scott, who seems not to have a very good understanding of the American constitutional system, obstinately refused. And, of course, another lawsuit was filed in an effort to rein in Scott.

RESTORATION OF FELONS' RIGHT TO VOTE: Enlightened states reinstate a felon's civil rights automatically upon completion of his or her prison sentence. Florida, however, currently has approximately 95,000 citizens waiting for a hearing to have their rights restored, which includes the right to serve on a jury, to run for public office, and to vote. Under new rules adopted in March 2011 by Gov. Scott and his cabinet, the wait for a hearing is now a minimum of seven years, and in reality so lengthy that in all likelihood most felons will never get to vote again. A recent report by the Florida Parole Commission found that felons whose civil rights have been reclaimed are much more likely to be integrated back into society and less likely to commit new crimes, but Scott, who opposes automatic restoration of ex-convicts' rights, believes "We ought to have a process where people apply. That's the biggest thing from my standpoint." Exactly what to make of that statement is anyone's guess. Most recently, between January and April 2012, almost 7,000 felons were removed from voter rolls in Florida. Among these, 51 percent were registered Democrats, 17 percent Republicans, and the rest had no affiliation. One wonders if such numbers also figure in Scott's calculations?

To sum up, here are a couple of sane voices concerning voter suppression activities by the Scott administration. Florida state Sen. Arthenia Joyner: "It is un-American to make it a burden to vote. Too many people fought and died for this right"; and former Florida Gov. Charlie Crist: "Good government begins with the voter, and creating barriers to voter registration or access to the polls is contrary to our democratic ideals . . . . Florida should be doing all it can to promote more voter participation, not creating barriers to it."

ENVIRONMENT AND ENERGY

The key issues: 1) Growth management and land development; 2) Management of Florida's water; 3) Everglades restoration project; 4) Privatization of Florida's water; and 5) Energy policy.

Generally speaking, Rick Scott failed spectacularly during his first 16 months in office to protect Florida's environment. Instead of working to conserve and preserve, the governor, in league with pro-development forces in the Florida Legislature, did just about everything possible to undo a generation or more of progress aimed at safeguarding Florida's most precious natural resources, especially water and environmentally sensitive land. All signs indicate the outlook for the next 32 months—Scott's remaining time in office—will be just as bleak or even bleaker for the future of the state's environment. One of the saddest aspects of all this is that relatively few citizens realize the extent of the damage Scott and his fellow extremists have already done to Florida's natural heritage.

Scott talks a good line about how much he yearns for a green Florida, but his deeds paint quite a different picture. Here's one small, though telling, example of how he really feels about environmental issues: In October 2011, he had a seat to fill on the Florida Fish and Wildlife Conservation Commission, a state organization that deals with fresh and saltwater fishing, hunting, protecting endangered species, and enforcing conservation laws. The agency has nearly 2,000 full-time employees and an annual budget of some millions of dollars. Twenty people applied for the job. Two of the applicants had served previously on the commission, another was president of a prominent sportsman's group, another a vice president of the Florida Wildlife Federation, another headed an animal rescue organization, and yet another was a former Humane Society investigator.

Did Scott choose one of these potentially well-qualified people to serve on the commission? No. Instead he picked Charles W. "Chuck" Roberts III, a paving contractor located in Northwest Florida whose company has a lengthy record of violating environmental regulations, including improper storage of chemicals, chemical spills, a storage tank that leaked diesel fuel, and a facility that generated excessive air pollution. Obviously Mr. Roberts is a fellow in business to make all the money he can, and if environmental issues get in the way, tough luck. When questions arose about Scott's choice, the governor's press secretary said with a straight face, "Gov. Scott and his appointments staff felt he [Roberts] was the best qualified for the position." And in a twisted way, this was true. Remember Scott's double-negatived comment after becoming governor: "I'm not going to appoint people that don't believe what I believe in"?

GROWTH MANAGEMENT AND LAND DEVELOPMENT: After only a few months as governor, Scott eagerly signed a bill into law that eradicated more than a quarter of a century of reasonably effective growth management legislation in Florida. Specifically, the new law repealed the 1985 landmark legislation (officially the Local Government Comprehensive Planning Act) that, among other things, required developers to take into account the impact of their construction projects on local communities and their environment. In other words, a basic concept embedded in the 1985 law was "concurrency," meaning roads, water and sewer systems, police and fire services, parks, etc. had to be planned for or in place as new developments were being constructed—an indisputably sane idea.

Those who fought to retain the 1985 law pulled no punches. Charles Pattison, president of the organization 1000 Friends of Florida, a nonprofit group established to serve as "a watchdog over growth management in Florida," exemplified the strong, widespread opposition to Scott's new policies. Pattison slammed the governor and his enablers in the Legislature as greedy, shortsighted pawns of influential developers: "What has happened? Florida's leaders are supporting short-term gain over long-term, sustainable economic prosperity. They view this state as nothing more than a commodity, to be bought and sold to the highest bidder regardless of consequences. This harks back to the anything-goes days of the 1960s and 1970s when the Everglades burned, untreated sewage poured into the Gulf of Mexico, and local taxpayers footed the bill for roads and sewer systems for unneeded new development" (*St. Petersburg Times*, June 12, 2011).

In addition to approving the gutting of the 1985 growth management law, Scott, in his 2011-12 budget, could not spare even one dime for the highly successful Florida Forever land conservation program that in past years had received up to $300 million in bonded funding. In his 2012-13 budget, he relented and included $8 million for Florida Forever, which might sound like a lot of money but actually it was just a bit more than the $5 million he allocated for a private rowing club in Sarasota County to have a regatta.

MANAGEMENT OF FLORIDA'S WATER: Water, such a common liquid, is taken for granted by most Americans, unless they happen to live in a perpetually drought-prone area. Florida happens to be awash in water, being a subtropical peninsula surrounded by a mighty ocean on one side and a massive gulf on the other with a multitude of bays, rivers, lakes, streams, springs, aquifers, swamps, and ponds within its perimeter. In Florida it's unheard of to live more than a short distance from a substantial body of water. Water sustains life: We drink it, cook with it, bathe in it, flush away waste with it, clean things from dishes to clothes to vehicles with it, swim and play in it, travel on it, irrigate with it. The list goes on. And let's not forget, freshwater is relatively inexpensive and so abundant that Floridians squander lots of it every day.

What most citizens of Florida rarely sense or think about is the complex scientific and economic networks that facilitate daily access to the clean water people need and use. Beginning after the end of World War II, long before Rick Scott arrived on the scene, the Florida Legislature wisely created five regional water management districts (WMDs) covering the entire state, each divided along not political but hydrologic boundaries. While WMD policies have traditionally been set by boards comprised of local citizens appointed by Florida's governor, the day-to-day work of the agencies is done by professional staffs responsible for determining how much freshwater for residential and commercial use can be drawn from rivers, lakes, and underground springs at any given time without stressing the natural environment. The main mission of the WMDs is to ensure that all Floridians have enough usable water to satisfy their everyday needs. This includes providing reclaimed (or treated) wastewater used as a substitute for freshwater to water lawns, wash vehicles, and irrigate agricultural land. The WMDs are also tasked with acquiring and protecting wetlands as well as helping to prevent floods.

All of this business of course costs money, and the WMDs, until recently, received the bulk of their funding from voter created "special taxing districts" established to support their work. The special taxing district concept makes it possible for property taxes to fund any number of specific community needs, for example housing for the poor or mosquito control programs or public libraries or, in the case of WMDs, professional management of the regional water supply.

From the very beginning of his governorship, Rick Scott had his eye on Florida's special taxing districts. Remember his comment soon after being sworn in: "It is no different than when I took over companies. One of the first things you have to do is get control of the checkbook." In the spring of 2011 the Florida Legislature, encouraged by the governor, for the first time granted itself the power to oversee WMD budgets, which led to spending caps. The following year Scott issued an executive order requiring his budget office to scrutinize the spending practices of all 1,615 special taxing districts in the state. Scott said he was looking for ways "to save taxpayer money and increase accountability." In reality, he was looking for ways to take control of some of the larger, more politically sensitive projects being funded via special taxing districts—and the five WMDs were prime targets. Since the beginning of their existence, the WMDs operated under the aegis of the state's Department of Environmental Protection, but for as long as anyone can remember, they conducted most of their business free from close oversight, principally because they carried out their responsibilities in a professional and efficient manner.

However, the arrival of Gov. Scott and his obsession with money and power drastically weakened how the WMDs function. During the first 16 months of his governorship, the five agencies witnessed draconian cuts in their budgets, which in turn led to the loss of many employees at both the administrative and field levels, the latter including seasoned hydrologists and other scientists with years of creditable experience dealing with public water concerns. One of the governor's new appointees, Blake Guillory, who took over as executive director of the Southwest Florida WMD in the fall of 2011, fired most of his top aides before he even spent a single day in his new office. Asked why, he said the people he let go "didn't fit." Later it was learned that Guillory, an engineer, had no previous experience running a governmental agency but was good at taking orders. Just the kind of executive director Scott wanted.

As might be guessed, Scott's intervention crimped the WMDs' traditional nonpartisan autonomy, specifically reducing their decision-making capability and reliance on hydrologists and other scientifically trained personnel. In a word, the work of Florida's water management districts was quickly becoming politicized. Major decisions would now be made in Tallahassee by the governor and his staff along with appointees like Blake Guillory, key conservative Republican legislators, and a bunch of representatives from private industries whose fortunes were tied to the use of lots of the people's freshwater. This was all happening behind closed doors where Florida's top water polluters (phosphate miners, cement producers, paper manufacturers, sugar cane farmers, etc.) were in Scott's corner cheering his every move, knowing that he and his administration would do very little if anything to try to curb their businesses from fouling the state's waterways.

Environmentalists and professionals who understand Florida's water issues were appalled. They were aware that agricultural and industrial concerns consume roughly 90 percent of Florida's freshwater. "It's a dark day for Florida's water resources," observed Charles Lee, speaking for the Florida Audubon Society. Tom Swihart, a former administrator at the Florida Department of Environmental Protection and author of the book *Florida's Water: A Fragile Resource in a Vulnerable State* (RFF Press, 2011), writes, "Big cuts to water management district budgets will prevent many Florida water problems from being solved. But over the long run, the centralization of water management power in Tallahassee will do even more harm. Citizens no longer have meaningful access to water management decision-making. Tallahassee does not know best." Victoria Tschinkel, secretary of the Florida Department of Environmental Protection for six years when Bob Graham was governor, noted that Scott "was talking about all their [WMDs'] money and their taxing authority" during his first week in Tallahassee, adding it seemed clear to her Scott "wants control over the water supply in Florida."

And Mark Howard, in an editorial in *Florida Trend* (January 2012) commenting on Scott's "evisceration" of the state's WMDs, points out, "The districts were bloated and even more self-righteous than Scott, but they've done a commendable job of ensuring water supply during decades of explosive growth. Most important, they insulated critical water-use decisions from the political meddling that's the Legislature's stock and trade. They remain the most sensible of Florida's various regulatory mechanisms—organized regionally, with boundaries that match what they were intended to manage: Florida's hydrology . . . . Scott has politicized the water management process and sent a signal that he didn't understand the importance of Florida's natural environment to its economic health and didn't much care."

EVERGLADES RESTORATION PROJECT: Though Gov. Scott is afflicted with poor enunciation, he has no trouble issuing written statements full of cheerful rhetoric as clear as it is empty. And nowhere is his rhetoric emptier than on the subject of Florida's Everglades, a unique 9,000-square-mile water system that flows approximately 225 miles starting from the rivers and marshlands north of Lake Okeechobee in Central Florida to the bottom of the state where it empties into Florida Bay. Marjorie Stoneman Douglas's classic book, *The Everglades: River of Grass,* first published in 1947, tells the story not only of the Everglades' unique ecological value to all Florida's citizens but also its vital hydrologic contribution as the main source of freshwater for Miami and the rest of South Florida. Regrettably, for decades the Everglades have been ailing, suffering from pollution owing to nutrient-rich agricultural runoffs, toxic pesticides, sewage effluents, and salt water intrusion. The Glades have also been damaged by dikes, dams, and canals that have drained portions of what Douglas called a "river of grass." Another assault has come from urban land developers who constantly scheme to push back the natural boundaries of the Glades, annexing portions of it to create new towns and cities far to the west of Miami and Fort Lauderdale.

Gov. Scott did not create these problems. However, aside from pretty words ("My administration is absolutely focused on making sure the right thing happens with the Everglades"), he's done very little to help push forward a long-delayed joint federal-state project to revitalize the Everglades, an undertaking that requires a huge financial commitment.

What has Scott done so far?

First, his initial budget (2011-12) proposed an investment of roughly $20 million, a drop in the bucket; his second budget doubled that amount, but $40 million is still pitiful considering the needs of the Everglades and its central place in Florida's history, geography, economy, and hydrology. Other recent Florida governors have annually budgeted between $100 million and $200 million for the Everglades restoration project. Second, in October 2011, Scott went to the nation's capital to inform the U.S. Interior Department that the state needed six more years to work on cleaning up pollution flowing into the Glades. The original deadline had been 2012, then it was moved to 2016, and now it's 2022—that is, if U.S. District Judge Alan Gold agrees. He's previously indicated his great displeasure with the obvious foot-dragging on the Glades project. Scott, of course, told officials in Washington what they wanted to hear, that "A healthy Everglades is part of a healthy Florida economy." Third and last, remember how Scott and the Legislature slashed the budgets of the state's water management districts? The largest and most prominent of the five WMDs is the South Florida district because it serves the most people and it deals with the Everglades. Unfortunately, under Scott, the budget cuts the South Florida WMD suffered has led to a downgrading of its credit rating, which in turn has negatively affected work on restoration of the Everglades.

PRIVATIZATION OF FLORIDA'S WATER: No one (yet) has proposed privatizing all of Florida's water, but in the 2012 session of the Legislature a bill was introduced that suggests Floridians might soon be hearing more about the possibility, especially given Gov. Scott's compulsion to privatize practically all government functions. The privatization effort came in the form of a Republican bill introduced in the Florida House of Representatives that would designate reclaimed wastewater as a commodity that could be brought and sold to the highest bidder. Currently, once wastewater is treated, it comes under the control of the publicly administered water management districts to be allocated on a per need basis around the state. Former governor Bob Graham vigorously opposed the bill, stating, "The history in Florida is that water belongs to the people of Florida wherever it is and under whatever process it may be undergoing. It is a fundamental resource of all Floridians." Fortunately, reason prevailed, and the proposed bill was changed to indicate the public continues to own the wastewater it treats. But in the future this could change: Remember Victoria Tschinkel's warning that Scott "wants control over the water supply of Florida."

ENERGY POLICY: Gov. Scott was not in office when the Deepwater Horizon oil rig, owned by Transocean and leased by British Petroleum (BP), exploded in the Gulf of Mexico on April 20, 2010, causing one of the worst environmental disasters in American history. He did, however, get involved a year later when BP was handing out reparations to the states whose economies were affected by the massive spill. Specifically, in April 2011, Scott announced a $30 million BP "grant" to be used to promote marketing and tourism in seven of Florida's Panhandle counties. At the time Scott thanked BP for "stepping up." What he didn't do was join other affected Gulf states (Louisiana, Alabama, etc.) in a federal lawsuit against Transocean—a suit that eventually might yield tens of billions of dollars in compensation for the states. Scott, who apparently never shrinks from provoking lawsuits, argued, "My goal is to try to work with BP and make sure we don't end up in litigation." Prominent trial attorney Steve Yerrid, then Florida's special counsel to deal with claims against BP and others responsible for the spill, responded by calling $30 million in this context "chump change"; he also suggested the governor was "simply too friendly with corporate America . . . . Scott does not want corporate America to pick up the check even when the wrongdoing is clear, the damages apparent and the need for payment never greater."

Despite the Deepwater Horizon catastrophe, Scott continues to support further drilling for oil and gas in the Gulf, which, given his ultraconservative views, does not surprise many people. What did surprise—and alarm—Florida's environmental community was a comment he made at a meeting of the Economics Club of Florida in Tallahassee when, responding to a question, he appeared to endorse increased exploration and drilling in the Big Cypress National Preserve, an enormous federal wildlife sanctuary in the southwestern area of the state adjacent to the Everglades National Park and generally considered part of the Everglades system. Because he lived in that area of Florida prior to moving to Tallahassee, Scott was most likely aware that oil and other natural resources were currently being extracted in parts of the preserve. What he apparently did not know is that, since 1974 when the U.S. government acquired the land from the Collier family, federal law has prohibited commercial development in the Big Cypress; only Collier companies that had established petroleum and mining interests in the preserve before the sale of the land are permitted to continue to operate.

Environmentalists constantly watch to make sure no other energy interests are allowed to operate in the Everglades. The goal is to save this unique natural asset, not exploit it. Kirk Fordham, then head of the Everglades Foundation, a nonprofit created specifically to protect the Glades and adjacent areas, issued a stern warning: "My suggestion to the governor is quite simple. Don't go there . . . . he should abandon any notion of encouraging drilling in this sacred place." Very quickly, Scott's office issued a statement backing off the notion of expanding drilling anywhere in the Everglades, saying that is "not on the table."

Another energy question Scott dealt with around this time involved energy-efficiency standards proposed by Florida's Public Service Commission, the agency that regulates utility companies in the state. Scott opposed stricter efficiency standards because they increase the cost of electricity for both residential and corporate consumers. This policy conflicted with Scott's goal of keeping energy costs low for Florida's businesses—and, just as important, for those businesses that might be considering moving, along with their jobs, to the state. This issue has yet to be resolved, but surely will be revisited in the near future.

Finally, Scott allowed a modest, bipartisan energy bill passed by the Legislature in the 2012 session to become law without his signature. Crafted by Adam Putnam, currently Florida's agriculture commissioner and a young man thought by many to have a good shot at eventually becoming governor of the state, the law is designed to move Florida toward greater energy diversity by promoting renewable sources as an alternative to fossil fuels. The law includes tax incentives totaling $100 million over a five-year period to encourage increased production of renewable energy, such as solar, wind, and biofuels, as well as the development of technology necessary to make renewables competitive. Unfortunately for Scott, the law posed a conflict: His popular agriculture commissioner authored the legislation whereas his good friends on the extreme right of the Republican party strongly opposed it. Leading the opposition was Americans for Prosperity, the Koch brothers think tank, which lambasted the bill as "crony capitalism" and the "opposite of free enterprise." See *First Coast News* (Florida Trend Online, April 11, 2012) for coverage of the Koch rant.

GAMBLING

Gov. Scott stayed out the major debate about gambling that took place during the 2012 session of the Florida Legislature. Highly controversial, the question boiled down to this: Should the state approve the creation of Las Vegas-style "destination resort casinos" in South Florida? Though Scott did not declare where he stood on the matter, it's quite likely the issue will resurface at some point before his term expires, and doubtless he will have a big say. Three popular gambling venues have a stake in the debate's outcome : 1) Destination resort casinos; 2) Seminole Tribe casinos; and 3) Internet cafes.

DESTINATION RESORT CASINOS: Ever since Florida began attracting large numbers of tourists, dating from the 1920s forward, gambling (or "gaming") has been the source of a huge moral headache for those opposed to it. For those in the business and the players who love to try to beat the odds, there's not enough of it.

Anti-gambling folks suggest, perhaps exaggerating a wee bit, that Florida already has more types of legal gambling for those who want it than Las Vegas has hookers. There are the parimutuels—horses, dogs, and jai alai; there are also "racinos" in South Florida that offer both slot machines _and_ parimutuel races (hence racinos); there is a State-run Lottery; there are eight Indian casinos scattered around the state; there are more than a thousand so-called Internet cafes (also known as sweepstakes cafes); there are old-fashioned bingo parlors; there are cruises that offer off-shore betting. Those who track this sort of thing say Florida is the fourth largest gambling state in the U.S., though others dispute this, saying it depends on what's being counted and by whom. The reality is, there's a lot of gambling in Florida.

But what Florida does not have at the moment are what have come to be known as "destination resort casinos." These are extravagantly appointed, neon-lighted, Vegas-style complexes that include hotels, restaurants, bars, entertainment sites, high-end retail stores, perhaps art galleries, and, of course, casinos that attract vacationers, conventioneers, business moguls, high rollers, et al. from all over the world. One of the developers who lobbied the Florida Legislature in 2012 for authority to build three destination casinos in South Florida promised that they would create approximately 100,000 permanent jobs in the region, plus 50,000 high-paying construction jobs that would last for some years. That was enough to bring the pro-business group Associated Industries of Florida onboard. Moreover, the new casinos, it was said, would add some $10 billion to the state's economy and entice six million additional tourists to Florida every year.

Not everyone was buying what the gambling industry was selling. Beginning in 1978, three statewide referenda have rejected bringing full-fledged casinos to Florida. Some people's religious values led them to oppose any type of gambling, but casinos—note "sin" in the middle of the word—were the ultimate evil. Others feared that going the way of glitzy destinations like Las Vegas, Atlantic City, and Biloxi, Mississippi, would bring a heavy influx of organized crime, prostitution, and lots of other undesirable enterprises. In other words, they worried that big-time casinos would damage Florida's reputation as a "family friendly" destination. It's hardly a surprise that the Walt Disney Company in Orlando is one of the most vocal anti-casino voices in the debate. State Sen. Ellyn Bogdanoff, a Republican from Fort Lauderdale and a leading sponsor of the 2012 casinos legislation, retorted: "People do not go to South Florida to see Mickey Mouse. We have the strip club capital of the world in Tampa. We have not ruined our family-friendly image." On the other hand, John Stemberger, lobbyist for the conservative Florida Family Policy Council, warned, "We will not sit back idly as the gambling industry attempts to buy out Florida and her elected officials with the corrupting influence of gaming money."

The 2012 Florida Legislature spend a sizable chunk of its 60-day session debating the merits of destination resort casinos. Bills introduced in both the Senate and House called for awarding exclusive licenses to construct three $2 billion mega-resorts in Miami-Dade and Broward counties, the two units of state government where voters had already approved slot machines. Representatives of some of the world's biggest casino concerns—Gentling Americas, Las Vegas Sands, and Wynn Resorts—were on hands to promote their products. Colin Au, Gentling's president, was especially optimistic about what big-time casinos could do for Florida's economy; likewise, he dealt sharply with critics, causing some raised eyebrows when he used the word "bullshit" not once but twice when refuting anti-gambling sentiments.

In the end, the casino legislation was defeated, not by a dramatic vote in the House or Senate chambers, but quietly in a House committee room where the 15-member Business and Consumer Affairs Subcommittee could not muster eight votes to get the bill out of committee.

Almost immediately after the defeat, pro-gambling forces began planning to reverse the decision by means of a public referendum that would put the issue squarely in the hands of Florida voters. An article in the *South Florida Sun-Sentinel* (April 17, 2012) by Kathleen Haughney and Nick Sortal reported "After striking out in the Florida Legislature this spring, gambling interests appear to be taking steps to seek direct approval from the state's voters for building Las Vegas-sized casino resorts in South Florida. Tallahassee lawyer and political consultant John French filed paperwork last week with the state creating a Political Action Committee called 'New Jobs and Revenue for Florida'—with the purpose of holding a statewide constitutional referendum on gambling." Stay tuned.

SEMINOLE TRIBE CASINOS: One of the winners when the resort casino bill failed was the Seminole Indian Tribe that owns seven of the state's eight Indian casinos, a business that now grosses more than $2 billion annually. In 2010, when Charlie Crist was Florida's governor, the tribe negotiated a deal with the state that gave it exclusive rights to operate Vegas-style slot machines and table games, including baccarat and blackjack, in South Florida's two most populous counties, Miami-Dade and Broward, as well as at Seminole facilities outside South Florida. In return, the tribe guaranteed the state a minimum of $1 billion over a five-year period, beginning with two $150 million payments in 2010.

The agreement gave the Seminole Tribe a monopoly over the casino business in Florida—a monopoly that would have disappeared should the 2012 casino resort legislation been approved. Sen. Bogdanoff shrugged off the possibility of breaking the state's agreement with the tribe: "Monopolies," she said, "are a bad thing. Gaming monopolies are toxic." In any event, the Seminole Tribe, at least for the present, reigns supreme over Florida's casinos.

INTERNET CAFES: Another winner when the casino resort initiative died were Internet cafes, popular establishments that trace their origins back to bingo, though today it's computer-driven gambling via video machines. Both the House and Senate versions of the casino bill would have put the cafes, which number more than a thousand in Florida, out of business. Also known as sweepstakes cafes or strip-mall casinos, Internet cafes cater largely to senior citizens and low income people, and unlike the parimutuels, racinos, and Indian casinos, they are not regulated by the state. Critics charge Internet cafes are "cheesy gambling joints" that ripoff the poor, whereas cafe owners say computers determine who wins and who loses, similar to the way the Florida Lottery operates. One thing is clear: Internet cafes are under siege in the Sunshine State.

P.S. GOV. SCOTT STIFFS COMPULSIVE GAMBLERS: As noted earlier, Scott did not take part in the great debate over destination resort casinos, at least not publicly, but he did make one sneaky move in the area of gambling during his first 16 months in office. When the Florida Legislature agreed in 2008 to allow slot machines into counties that approved having them, lawmakers mandated that every licensed casino and racino with slots must contribute $250,000 annually to the nonprofit Florida Council on Compulsive Gambling, an organization devoted to helping addicted gamblers deal with their problem. This procedure worked very well until Scott came along and unilaterally broke the deal by denying the council its money (currently about $900,000 annually); instead he put the money in the state's "rainy-day fund." (See Mary Ellen Klas's article "Gaming promises often exceed payoff" in the *St. Petersburg Times*, November 21, 2011.) Naturally, the good work of the council has suffered. When asked to defend the move, Scott brushed off the question by replying, "You have to make choices."

GUNS AND GUN CONTROL

In certain circles, Florida is known as the "gunshine state," meaning that the ultraconservative National Rifle Association (NRA) has a lock on drafting and passing gun legislation in the Sunshine State. So intimidating is the NRA that most Florida politicians have dropped the words "gun control" from their vocabulary. Predictably, Gov. Scott makes no bones about being an avid admirer of the Second Amendment, and during his first 16 months in office he supported every gun proposal the NRA made.

The major issues: 1) The right of physicians to discuss gun ownership with their patients or their families; 2) The controversial "stand your ground" law; and 3) A law that prohibits Florida municipal and county governments from enacting gun control ordinances.

DOCTORS, PATIENTS, AND GUN OWNERSHIP: In 2011 the Florida Legislature passed a bill entitled "Privacy of Firearm Owners" that states physicians and other licensed healthcare practitioners working in Florida "should refrain from making a written inquiry or asking questions concerning the ownership of a firearm or ammunition by the patient or by family members of the patient." In June Gov. Scott obediently signed this incredibly intrusive and censorious piece of legislation into law, another boneheaded decision. Very quickly the law was challenged in court, and in September a federal judge blocked its implementation, noting healthcare professionals have a First Amendment right to ask their patients about firearms and their availability in the home, especially when children are involved. The law's sponsor in the Legislature was aggrieved, asking "What's more important: the First Amendment or the Second Amendment? I thought a judge should value all the amendments to the Constitution." (This is the type of people who get elected to the Legislature in Florida.) Scott, undeterred by the judge's ruling, vowed to appeal. That's where the issue remains today.

FLORIDA'S "STAND YOUR GROUND" LAW: Gov. Scott was not in office in 2005 when the "stand your ground" bill was passed by the Florida Legislature, the House voting for it by a wide margin and the Senate approving it unanimously. The honor of signing it into law belonged to former Gov. Jeb Bush, who did the deed as the NRA's top lobbyist literally patted him on the shoulder. The law, part of the NRA's campaign to expand gun rights across the nation, stipulates that anyone threatened with harm need not back off, or retreat, but rather has the legal right to stand and defend one's self, using lethal force if necessary, as long as the person wounded or killed is not a police officer. Many opposed passage of this ambiguous law, including law enforcement officers and gun control advocacy groups such as the Brady Campaign to Prevent Gun Violence.

In 2012 the law burst into the national consciousness with the tragic shooting death of Trayvon Martin, a young African American who was walking home alone and unarmed from a convenience store while visiting his father in Sanford, Florida. George Zimmerman, the man who killed Martin, was a neighborhood watch volunteer who had a permit to carry a concealed weapon. For reasons that remain unclear, Zimmerman pursued Martin despite being told not to and later, after the shooting, claimed he had been attacked. Using the "stand your ground" law as a defense, Zimmerman was released without being charged with a crime by the Sanford police. After weeks of waiting in vain for some action to be taken against their son's killer, Trayvon Martin's parents spoke out, instantly sparking something resembling a national crusade to achieve justice for Trayvon, and all young black males who are frequently subjected to unwarranted harassment by law enforcement officers. As pressure mounted on officials to do something, Gov. Scott named a well-regarded state attorney, Angela Corcy, to serve as the case's special prosecutor. Eventually, Zimmerman was charged with second degree murder and then released on bail to await trial, which will most likely occur in 2013.

Scott also appointed a task force, chaired by Jennifer Carroll, the state's lieutenant governor, to review the provisions and validity of the "standard your ground" law, which has come under withering criticism in Florida and around the country as the facts of the case became known. The task-force concept was doubtless a good idea, but once again the governor "stepped in it," this time with the help of Carroll, when assembling the 17-member group. "We have tapped a diverse and qualified group to carefully review our laws and our policies," said Scott, whose understanding of the word "diverse" was immediately challenged by practically everyone except the pro-gun lobby. The problem: Scott and Carroll included many prominent backers of "stand your ground" on the task force while failing to include any of its most vocal critics. As so often happens, this mulish governor had no interest in, or tolerance for, diverse opinions about the law or his policies. Research on the subject tells us successful leaders surround themselves with people who are not sycophants—what real leaders want are staffers and colleagues who offer a broad range of ideas and perspectives prior to decisions being made. Scott, on the other hand, acts as if he knows it all. He is, after all, the governor who said, "I'm not going to appoint people that don't believe what I believe in." The appointments to the so-called "task force" certainly underscore that dense attitude.

A final note: Special prosecutor Corey has opposed releasing public evidence concerning the case prior to going to trail, a legal position that conflicts with the state's public records law. To correct this so-called "problem," She has suggested the Florida Legislature change the law to suppress all evidence until a trial begins. (For more information, see Open Government and Public Records, pp. 000.)

LAW PROHIBITING LOCAL ORDINANCES REGARDING FIREARMS: During August 27-30, 2012, the Florida city of Tampa is scheduled to host the Republican National Convention, and naturally Tampa's mayor and his advisers were concerned about making the city as safe as possible for everyone involved. Toward that end, a long list of items not permitted in a wide area around the convention center was issued. These items include clubs, hatchets, shovels, switchblades, slingshots, and guns that shoot water and paint. Oddly missing from this catalog of potential weapons were handguns and other firearms that could cause much greater harm or mayhem than anything on the list.

Why was that? Were Tampa's elected officials so spacey they forgot about guns that shoot bullets? Well, no. Here's why guns weren't on the list: In 2011 Gov. Scott signed into law an NRA-composed bill passed by the Florida Legislature that took away the traditional right of municipal and county governments to enact ordinances regulating firearms in their jurisdictions. In other words, the city of Tampa did not have the authority to ban guns, even temporarily, outside the convention hall where the Republican candidates, delegates, and distinguished guests would be possible targets. Anyone with a permit to carry a concealed weapon—and at last count almost one million Floridians possess such permits—was welcome to come to the city armed and go anywhere. except inside the convention hall, where the secret service trumped Gov. Scott and the Florida Legislature.

Tampa's mayor, Bob Buckhorn, called the situation "absolutely insane . . . . The absurdity of banning squirt guns but not being able to do anything about real guns is patently obvious." Buckhorn asked Gov. Scott to issue an executive order banning firearms in downtown Tampa during the convention, but Scott refused. In a letter to the mayor, he wrote, "It is unclear how disarming *law-abiding* citizens would better protect them from the 'dangers and threats posed by those who would flout the law.' It is at just such times that the constitutional right to self-defense is most precious and must be protected from government overreach." Earlier, the *New York Times* in an editorial published on April 5, 2012, provided this take on the situation: "Political leaders mindful of public safety should be able to solve Tampa's gun control problem. But there's scant few of them in the [Florida] statehouse. The scene developing in Tampa is a national embarrassment that spotlights how timorous American politicians are before the gun lobby."

HEALTHCARE AND HEALTH INSURANCE

Of course Gov. Scott, after spending years building a huge chain of for-profit hospitals, knows a tremendous amount about how the American healthcare system functions—knowledge and experience that could be of real benefit to the people of Florida. Regrettably, so far, that's not been the case. Along with the knowledge and experience, Scott brought a set of rigid conservative political biases to the governorship that do not bode well for future of Florida's many citizens who are sick, elderly, disabled, or poor. Indeed, during his first 16 months in office, the governor brought only negative energy to the big issues he dealt with concerning Florida's healthcare: 1) The Patient Protection and Affordable Care Act; 2) Medicaid 3) Shrinking budgets, shrinking care; and 4) Deregulation of nursing homes and assisted living facilities.

PATIENT PROTECTION AND AFFORDABLE CARE ACT: Scott's antagonism toward President Obama's healthcare reform legislation, derided as "Obamacare," is well-known. No matter what its fate in the U.S. Supreme Court, the Patient Protection and Affordable Care Act, which became the law of the land in March 2010, is the first comprehensive effort in a generation to overhaul the country's arcane healthcare system. In Scott's mind, however, the law was "not the law," and he arrogantly refused federal money to prepare for its implementation, an action that represented supercilious and probably impeachable behavior. The governor believes, along with some other hard-core conservatives, that President Obama's program is a plot to take the country down the road to "socialized medicine."

One of the provisions of the law that obviously stuck in the governor's craw concerns cracking down on Medicare waste and fraud. As Kathleen Sebelius, Secretary of the U.S. Department of Health and Human Services, has pointed out, the law increases "penalties for criminals who steal from Medicare and it puts more law enforcement on the ground to find them." Perhaps if this law had been in effect back in 1997 when the Columbia/HCA scandal broke and Scott was forced to resign as the company's president and CEO, he would be in prison today instead governor of Florida.

One of main reasons—if not the reason—that Scott decided to run for governor in 2010 was to have as prominent a position as possible to lead the fight against the Patient Protection and Affordable Care Act. And in fact during Scott's first 16 months as the state's governor, Florida has been at the forefront of vigorously opposing the new healthcare law as it has wended its way through various lower courts. Should the U.S. Supreme Court, which held hearings in March 2012 and is expected to rule on the law's constitutionality in June, find it unconstitutional, you can be certain there will be much celebrating at the Governor's Mansion in Tallahassee.

MEDICAID: Gov. Scott's 2012-13 budget secured draconian cuts ($2 billion) in the state's share of Medicaid spending, an action that adversely affects the quality of patient care for some of Florida's weakest and poorest citizens, including children. But get this, some of the money saved by reducing Medicaid funding was used to add $1 billion to the education budget, which Scott had cut the previous year by $1.3 billion. Suddenly the governor realized Florida needs a decent educational system to help attract out-of-state businesses to relocate in Florida, so he might be able to meet his campaign commitment to bring 700,000 new jobs to the state in seven years. This is obviously no way to run a state government. Rather, it's called a con man's trick, a shell game. And as for those citizens who rely on Medicaid—tough luck.

The governor's approach to Medicaid, according to an experienced Florida hospital administrator, is "to chip away at the program's integrity" by denying it adequate funding. In 2011 the state began carrying out a policy of privatizing care for long-term Medicaid patients by moving them into for-profit managed care facilities, and current plans call for starting to shift other Medicaid beneficiaries into managed care by 2113. Federal health officials require that Florida's managed care companies and health maintenance organizations (HMOs) spend at least 85 percent of the funds they receive on patient care. The bottom line, however, is the private companies involved will make money, the state will save money, and patients will inevitably get screwed by receiving a reduction in medical services. Does this sound familiar? Isn't this much like what occurred when Columbia/HCA's for-profit hospitals under Scott's direction squeezed every penny of profit it could out of each unit by reducing the quality of care? Rick Scott, what a guy. We're talking here about a man who worships only one metric, and that's money. Too bad compassion can't be monetized—if it could, Rick might value compassion more than his sorry record shows he does.

Speaking of lack of compassion and empathy, Scott saw to it that Medicaid reimbursement rates for hospitals were significantly reduced during his early months in office, creating hardships for patients and hospitals alike. In another controversial move, in 2012 Scott and the Legislature teamed up to pressure Florida's 67 counties to pay some $325 million to settle disputed billing claims under the state's Medicaid cost-sharing law—this even though the counties had persuasive arguments they didn't owe anywhere near that amount. But Scott wanted the money and wanted it now, ignoring evidence of accounting errors and stories of double and triple billing most likely caused by a faulty software system used by the state. As a prod to get the counties to pay up, the Legislature passed and Scott signed a bill authorizing the state to garnish cost-sharing funds from the counties for Medicaid services for the next five years until the backlogged bills are paid. The last word heard on this subject was that the Florida Association of Counties, representing 47 of the state's counties, had decided to sue the state concerning resolution of the matter.

SHRINKING BUDGETS, SHRINKING CARE: Over the 16-month period covered here, Scott and his pals in the Legislature managed to either significantly cut the budget for many vital healthcare facilities and programs or to do away them entirely. A few examples: The highly regarded A.G. Holley tuberculosis hospital in Palm Beach County, the last such hospital of its kind in Florida, was shuttered and a subsequent TB outbreak was covered up for months . . . . The Florida State Hospital in Chattahoochee, for more than 60 years the state's premier hospital serving patients with serious mental illnesses, lost 140 employees, and 160 more were reduced to part-time status . . . . The Florida Department of Health suffered budget cuts affecting programs that promote the health of women, including one that provided contraceptive services to low-income families . . . . The Florida Agency for Persons with Disabilities experienced "unconscionable cuts of up to 40 percent" for treatment of Floridians who are developmentally disabled . . . . Funding to test for severe combined immune deficiency (SCID) when screening newborns for genetic diseases was vetoed by the governor. This list only scratches the surface of what's happening to healthcare in Florida under the reign of Rick Scott.

DEREGULATION OF NURSING HOMES AND ASSISTED LIVING FACILITIES: Florida has the highest percentage of residents 65 and over than any state (17.3%), and therefore it's no surprise Florida also has hundreds of nursing homes (technically called skilled nursing and rehabilitation facilities) and thousands of assisted living facilities (ALFs). Also not surprising, this industry, which grows larger each year due to the aging of the baby-boomer population, has strong lobbies in Tallahassee that look out for the interests of those who own and manage the state's nursing homes and ALFs. But who looks out for the interests of the residents and patients, people who are normally either frail or ill and often alone or ignored by busy relatives? It's a scenario that inevitably invites exploitation and abuse—and these twin evils occur in nursing homes and ALFs more often than most of us care to know.

Back in the 1970s and '80s, in response to well-publicized instances of mistreatment of nursing home and assisted living residents, the federal and Florida state governments adopted a series of strong regulations aimed at putting a stop to the worst abuses. Among the safeguards enacted during that reformist period was the Long-term Care Ombudsman Program that encourages local volunteers to monitor the quality of care residents receive and to serve as advocates for those who have complaints. The ombudsman program continues today, though over time the industry has managed to undermine its effectiveness.

Enter Gov. Scott, who is more than willing to accommodate nursing home and ALF owners, managers, and lobbyists. High on their agenda was getting rid of the head of the statewide ombudsman program, 39-year-old reform-minded Brian Lee, who had served in that position under Scott's two Republican predecessors, Jeb Bush and Charlie Crist. In the opinion of nursing home and ALF industry brass, Lee took his job much too seriously. An honest man who couldn't be controlled or co-opted or bought off by the industry, Lee sincerely believed in protecting the weak from the strong. When word got to the new governor that those who own and manage Florida's nursing homes and ALF facilities wanted Lee gone, it didn't take long for Scott to issue him an ultimatum: resign or be fired.

Scott must have slept well that evening: Another burdensome and frivolous regulation, the ombudsman program, had been dealt another blow.

IMMIGRATION

Unlike Arizona and Alabama, states that recently enacted harsh laws against immigrants, Florida did not pass any significant legislation in this area during Gov. Scott's first 16 months in office, though he campaigned on a promise to push for enactment of an Arizona-style law in Florida. Obviously, other issues took priority and, truth be told, there had not been a great clamor in recent years for action on illegal immigration in the state for several reasons. One was the Great Recession had dried up many of the jobs illegals were drawn to and they stopped entering the state in large numbers, at least for the time being. Also, the state's agricultural industry preferred a plan to make it legally permissible for illegal immigrants to work in the state's fields during harvesting season—the general perception being few Americans are willing to do this kind of work at today's rates. Lastly, the majority of Floridians appears to accept the fact that immigration is a federal, not a state, responsibility.

The only immigration issue Gov. Scott dealt with directly since taking office was issuing an executive order (EO) in 2011 requiring every state employee's immigration status to be checked against a federal database called E-Verify. His order also included checking the status of employees of private companies that have contracts that do work for the state. "If somebody is in our country illegally, and they are violating our laws, we ought to be able to ask them if they're legal or not," Scott told a reporter. "That's what I'd like to have happen." But the governor's EO had to be amended when he learned federal law allows E-Verify to be used only for new hires. It was also determined the database is not always accurate or up-to date. In 2012 Scott pressed the Legislature to pass a bill along the lines of his EO, but the bill failed.

This note on immigration issues in Florida would not be complete without mentioning the fact that the Florida Legislature, in its 2012 session, debated—and failed to pass—the so-called Dream Act. The act would have permitted illegal immigrants' undocumented children born in Florida (and therefore U.S. citizens) to pay in-state tuition rates when attending the state's public colleges and universities. Current law requires such students to pay out-of-state tuition, which is considerably higher than in-state. There were tears and dashed hopes when the Dream Act went down to defeat, and word on the street was Gov. Scott would have vetoed it if it had passed. On the positive front, a lawsuit has been filed challenging the policy of charging Florida residents who are U.S citizens non-resident rates for college tuition.

JOBS, JOB CREATION, AND UNEMPLOYMENT

In early January 2011 Rick Scott rode into Tallahassee on the strength of his personal fortune and a couple of catchy slogans having to do with the state's stalled economy, i.e., "Let's get to work," and "700,000 new jobs in seven years." The newbie governor was brimming with confidence. People were worried about job security and layoffs, concerns Scott could exploit. The plan: He would first lower, then eventually end, state taxes on corporations large and small. Low or no taxes plus other financial incentives would not only allow existing companies in the state to grow, it would encourage the creation of new companies, all of which would improve Florida's outlook concerning jobs. Moreover, Scott's pro-business policies would prompt many out-of-state companies to relocate in the Sunshine State, bringing with them jobs galore. Scott would also get rid of needless regulations that cut into a company's bottom line. And he would see to it that Florida's businesses had cheap energy and a state government ready to cater to their every need. Florida would blossom under the wise leadership of King Rick.

Of course Scott's aspirations turned out to be something of a pipe dream, a fantasy concocted by an oddly insensitive man who previously had never, not for a single moment, served in a public office anywhere. However, It didn't take long for the clueless Scott to realize that being head of a government was quite a different matter than being a corporate CEO or imperious autocrat. And though he always put the best gloss on both Florida's employment and unemployment numbers (just as he did the doughnut count in his second State of the State address), the Florida economy barely moved a tick in response to his ultraconservative policies. Only entrepreneurs and their top management enthusiastically endorsed Scott's platform of cake for corporatists and crumbs for everyone else. A cartoon by the *Miami Herald*'s Jim Morin (reprinted in the *Tampa Bay Times*, February 16, 2012) said it all: Scott is holding a placard that reads "FLORIDA IS OPEN FOR BUSINESS" as he speaks to a businessman seated behind a large desk. Says the governor, "Our schools are a wreck, we shredded the social safety net, public safety is endangered with police and firefighter layoffs, outdated infrastructure, dwindling environmental resources, insufficient public transportation, sky-high property insurance rates . . . But we're BUSINESS FRIENDLY!!!"

It was around this time that people began calling Scott's Florida "the Walmart state."

The key issues: 1) Jobs lost; 2) Job creation; 3) International opportunities; 4) Scott's job strategy for the future; 5) The numbers game; and 6) Unemployment.

JOBS LOST: Wherever he went around the state, Gov. Scott was introduced as Florida's "Jobs Governor." From the very beginning of his campaign in 2010, jobs-jobs-jobs had been Scott's signature issue. But despite all the hype, the governor's overall record on job creation during the first third of his four-year term left much to be desired. Consider this: Only 77,100 jobs were created in the state between January 2011 (the month Scott was inaugurated) and January 2012, and that number falls to an anemic 54,200 if Scott's first month in office is excluded. In fact, during Scott's first 16 months as governor his efforts on the jobs front often seemed to be more involved with losing jobs rather than gaining them.

Some examples:

*Using a hatchet, the governor chopped off some 3,500 state jobs in budgetary year 2011-12 and a bit more than that the following year.

*By slashing the budget for K-12 education in 2011-12 by $1.3 billion, he managed to put a goodly number of teachers, librarians, and educational aides on the unemployment rolls. Also, cuts in both the 2011-12 and 2012-13 budgets for Florida's public universities caused layoffs of a substantial number of educators and support personnel.

*Deep cuts in Medicaid funding in both Scott's budgets put many hospital employees out of work. Likewise, the University of Miami's medical school announced layoffs of hundreds of workers in the areas of administration and research beginning in the spring of 2012 as a result of losing millions of dollars in state funding. The Miami-based Jackson Health System suffered similar budget cuts.

*The nonprofit Jackson Laboratory, a multimillion-dollar biotech research facility based in Maine, expressed serious interest in moving its operation to Florida, first to Collier County and, when that didn't pan out, to the city of Sarasota and its University of South Florida campus. Finally, in the summer of 2011, after months of frustrating negotiations with Scott, Jackson gave up on Florida and moved its genomic research lab to the University of Connecticut's Health Center campus.

*In 2011 Clearwater, a major city on Florida's Gulf Coast, lost jobs when two important companies relocated in others states. The first, Inuvo Inc., a startup that produces analytical software for Internet users, moved its headquarters to New York City where the firm announced it would have access to the "best and brightest people"; the second, CCS Medical, one of area's largest private companies, was lured away to suburban Dallas, a move that very much pleased Scott's mentor, Texas Gov. Rick Perry.

*One of the most newsworthy loss of jobs in Florida during Scott's early months as governor occurred when, in November 2011, Solantic, a chain of healthcare clinics founded by none other than Scott himself, moved its corporate headquarters from Jacksonville in Florida to Nashville, Tennessee. Scott admitted disappointment: "I believe that we've put ourselves in a position that this [Florida] is the best state to build businesses. But some people, I guess, don't agree with me." (Note that Scott started Solantic in 2001 before he became governor, and was forced to sell the company after his election.)

*Without doubt the most devastating job loss for Florida happened soon after Scott became governor when he contemptuously—against the advice of practically everyone, including most people in the business community—rejected $2.4 billion from the federal government for the state to launch the first leg of a much needed national high-speed rail system. Scott's hubris cost Florida thousands and thousands of well-paying jobs, as well as destroying potential opportunity for future economic growth and development in every region of the state. Robyn Blumner, a *Tampa Bay Times* columnist, quotes disgusted businessman Bruce Goldman in a piece entitled "Scott derailed a Florida job express" (September 4, 2011) as saying, "You know, he [Scott] talked jobs, jobs, jobs, and then he took all those jobs away from the construction industry. There would have been so much more work, so much more money coming in from the Tampa-Orlando corridor and that just really hurt us." To add insult to injury, later Scott bragged about refusing the federal money at a Republican Governors Association meeting in Orlando. Playing to the wacko right-wing element, Scott sneered: "I apologize to anybody who came to this city to ride the high-speed rail project. I killed that."

JOB CREATION: What's obvious from the foregoing list of jobs lost is that when Scott talks about job creation, he's almost always talking about private sector jobs. Put another way, political leaders have only so many options when it comes to stimulating job growth, and Scott's chosen method is a two-pronged approach that conforms perfectly with his extreme right-wing political ideology: 1) Ruthlessly starve the public sector, and 2) Aggressively feed the private sector.

Unfortunately, creating and pursuing private sector jobs can be a dicey undertaking, especially in a sluggish, highly competitive global economy—the sort of economy Florida has been bogged down in for half a dozen or more years. Private sector jobs can either be grown at home or they can be imported from other states or abroad. But during a period of prolonged recession, such as the one the world is currently experiencing, there are normally not enough homegrown jobs coming on stream to offset those lost due to the weak economy. Attracting companies and their workforce to relocate therefore becomes the most feasible way for governments (national, state, county, municipal) to generate jobs and stem the tide of unemployment. But, as leaders like Scott have found out, importing jobs and job creators in bad economic times is not a simple matter of waving a wand: Those who have jobs to give want something valuable in return. It's a sellers' market.

What can government officials looking to import private sector jobs into their communities or states give to companies to induce them to relocate? Actually, there are a bunch of possible inducements: 1) Money in the form of cash, grants, and/or tax breaks; 2) Superior infrastructure, including buildings, power and water supplies, roads, public transportation, excellent telecommunications, schools, and libraries; and 3) Intangibles such as a highly skilled local workforce, good restaurants, theaters, sports facilities and teams, parks, beaches, and fine weather. In government-speak, all of the above items are called "incentives."

Gov. Scott learned (we hope) two fundamental lessons when he hung out his "FLORIDA IS OPEN FOR BUSINESS" sign, the first being that competition for imported private sector jobs, especially in a weak economy, is a cutthroat business that usually requires more incentives than just money; and the second being that Florida does not have an overabundance of incentives that impress most companies' top leadership and their employees. Realistically, all Scott has to offer companies willing to relocate are tax breaks and perhaps a little cash, both of which come at the expense of other incentives (such as underfunded educational institutions; inadequate public transportation; lack of the "best and brightest" workers). Of course, Florida also has a few enticing intangibles such as excellent beaches and lots of sunshine, but often that's not enough to carry the day when a company adds up an area's pluses and minuses. A letter on the subject from a reader, Joe Milberg, in the December 2011 issue of *Florida Trend,* concludes: "The only companies relocating to Florida under Gov. Scott and the current Legislature will be those who have not done their due diligence" (emphasis added.)

At one point Scott told a reporter he yearned to attract a major automaker like Audi to Florida. Apparently Volkswagen, which owns Audi, is planning to build an Audi plant somewhere, someday in the U.S. "It would be nice to have that one," Scott mused, but then he admitted the chances of such a coup were slim at best. When or if the Audi plant is built, there will be 50 U.S. states on the prowl for a company with Volkswagen's deep pockets. And there's one other nagging problem with incentives designed to lure companies away from one place to another: Financial incentives given by governments to private sector job creators frequently turn out to be bad deals for taxpayers. In too many instances, a company promises to provide X number of jobs in return for X millions of dollars in the form of upfront money or grants or generous tax breaks, or all three. Then, a couple of years later, said company is on the verge of bankruptcy, can't pay its employees, and is soon looking for the next sucker in the next state who will offer attractive "incentives" after the company restructures its debt. The literature on business incentives is full of such horror stories.

INTERNATIONAL OPPORTUNITIES: It's not surprising that in a global economy more than a quarter of a million Floridians work for foreign-owned companies either in Florida or abroad. Following in the footsteps of his recent predecessors, Gov. Scott and key members of his staff have undertaken a number of trade missions abroad, meeting with their counterparts in Canada, Brazil, Israel, Panama, and most recently Spain. The main goal is to expand international trade—the more trade, the more jobs. For example, Florida's major ports and their workers are beneficiaries of robust trade with foreign countries. (See the May 2012 issue of *Florida Trend* that carries a full-page ad on page 19 headlined "Florida Ports Equal Florida Jobs.") Robert Trigaux, writing in the *Tampa Bay Times* (September 4, 2011), does suggest Scott's people need to do more thorough advance work "so these trade missions come across less like high school field trips and more like substantive deal-cutting business events." In the recent mission to Spain, for instance, Scott met King Juan Carlos and embarrassed all concerned by blithering on and on about the monarch's shooting of an elephant on a trip to Botswana; apparently Scott was unaware that the elephant incident had been roundly denounced by the Spanish people and press, causing Juan Carlos considerable anguish.

SCOTT'S JOB STRATEGY FOR THE FUTURE: After months of experiencing mediocre numbers regarding job growth in Florida—growth that rarely exceeded the national average and frequently fell well below it—Gov. Scott decided to try a different tack. Quite obviously, promoting Florida as a state "OPEN FOR BUSINESS" wasn't attracting nearly the number of private sector jobs he had counted on. So, in October 2011, with appropriate fanfare, he launched his STEM initiative, which ideally links the high-paying jobs of tomorrow with the cutting-edge technical education of today. (STEM—an acronym for the academic disciplines of Science, Technology,

Engineering, and Mathematics—is also discussed in some detail under EDUCATION on pages 66-67.)

It's worth noting here, however, that the idea of linking STEM subjects with lucrative jobs has been around for years, and was actively promoted by former Florida Gov. Jeb Bush. Also, Scott provided no money for the state's colleges and universities to expand or enhance their STEM curricula . . . with one bizarre exception: The governor, along with a very determined state senator and a compliant Florida Legislature, created a 12th state university, Florida Polytechnic, whose course of study, as its name implies, will be devoted almost entirely to STEM subjects. The bizarre part of the story is that Florida Polytechnic, which is scheduled to open its doors in July 2012, currently lacks just about every component required of an institution of higher education, including accreditation. Most experienced educators suggest dear old Florida Poly cannot hope to achieve accreditation for at least eight or ten years, and probably it will take much longer.

Among Rick Scott's infamous muddleheaded decisions, Florida Poly ranks right up there with the rejection of the Tampa-Orlando high-speed rail project.

THE NUMBERS GAME: All politicians exaggerate their good numbers and downplay the negative ones. It comes with the territory. Gov. Scott, who ran for the office as a businessman and not a politician, puts most of the latter to shame when it comes to concocting flattering statistics to make himself look good; and conversely he has an uncanny (or perhaps psychopathic?) ability to deny or ignore those that make him look bad.

Among the most egregious examples of Gov. Scott's duplicity involves his well-known campaign promise to create "700,000 new jobs in seven years." At least twice during his campaign in 2010, he told reporters that the 700,000 jobs were in addition to an estimated one million new jobs economists predicted would be added to Florida's workforce over the seven-year period as a result of projected normal growth in the state. After discovering that job creation isn't as easy as falling off a log, Scott, instead of owning up to a miscalculation, lied. Specifically, when meeting with the *South Florida Sun-Sentinel* editorial board in the fall of 2011, Scott was asked, "Your pledge was for 700,000 [jobs] in addition to normal growth, wasn't it?" Scott replied, "No." Earlier, in August, a reporter asked him the same question: "No, that's not true" was the response. Possibly at the time Scott did not know that the press had video-taped evidence of him affirming that the 700,000 figure was indeed meant to be in addition to the one million projected jobs. Later, as the controversy refused to die, the beleaguered governor told another reporter, "I could argue that I don't have to create any jobs. I just have to make sure we don't lose jobs."

"Job CREATION"

It's this sort of behavior that makes it extremely difficult to believe anything Rick Scott says.

UNEMPLOYMENT: Florida's unemployment figures have come down substantially during Gov. Scott's first 16 months in office, dropping from a high of 12 percent in December 2010 when he was on the cusp of being inaugurated to 8.7 percent in April 2012. And even though the latest figure is higher than the national average, Scott's efforts to reduce unemployment in Florida have been heralded, by himself and others, as a great success. Actually, it's been a great success in sleight of hand, or legerdemain. That is, once again, Scott the con man, in league with the Florida Legislature's ultraconservative Republican leadership, has been busily scheming to deny jobless citizens their right to unemployment benefits. No wonder the numbers are going down.

Here's the poop: Scott's first attempt along these lines occurred when he signed a law requiring drug testing for welfare recipients, including those receiving unemployment benefits. That law has been declared unconstitutional, but there's little doubt it might have inhibited some people from applying for compensation they are entitled to. Later, new rules for those applying for unemployment benefits went into effect in August 2011—rules that have made it much more difficult for out-of-work Floridians to receive financial assistance. Some specifics: unemployment claims must now be filed online; applicants must complete a lengthy questionnaire regarding their job skills before receiving any assistance; those receiving benefits must go online every two week and provide evidence they have contacted ten prospective employers during that time, or go to a "one-stop" employment center and talk with a career counselor; and the state now has greater latitude to deny unemployment claims if "misconduct" at or outside of work contributed to loss of a job. For many Floridians—those who are older or for whom English is not their first language or who are not computer literate—these requirements present obstacles very difficult or impossible to overcome.

Have the new rules been effective in reducing the number of unemployment claims in Florida during the past 16 months? You bet. It's been reported that just three months after Scott and the Legislature started to squeeze the jobless in 2011, 65 percent of new unemployment claims were denied. Likewise, between August 2011 and April 2012, the Florida Department of Economics Opportunity, the agency that administers the unemployment program, has rejected 131,115 applicants based on failure to comply with one or more of the new requirements.

This is how Gov. Scott has reduced the unemployment rate in Florida he likes to brag about.

MINORITIES

Though more than 40 percent of Florida's approximately 19 million people identify themselves as Hispanic, African-American, or Asian, Gov. Scott largely avoided becoming involved in major issues concerning the state's minorities during his first 16 months in office. His selection of Jennifer Carroll, a black woman, as a running mate and ultimately lieutenant governor, provided a certain amount of insulation against any implications of racial or ethic bias, though Carroll appears to have had little impact on policymaking in the first third of Scott's four-year term. The record also indicates Scott included fewer minorities in the top three levels of his administration than had Charlie Crist, his predecessor. Also, some observers, including former Gov. Jeb Bush, were upset that soon after taking office Scott summarily fired three black women who had served honorably in previous administrations. Wrote Bush in an email to Scott: "I don't quite understand this decision. All three are African-Americans, non-political and good workers." Scott was not swayed. In another instance, the Florida Legislative Black Caucus publicly rebuked the governor for appointing too many "Scott clones" and not enough blacks as judges, but so far nothing much has come of that issue.

Others instances involving Scott and minorities:

*He campaigned promising Florida a tough Arizona-style immigration law, but as of April 2012 that legislation, which would most directly affect Hispanics, has not materialized. (See IMMIGRATION, pages 86 for additional information.)

*In 2011 Scott approved a controversial Republican-sponsored bill ostensibly aimed at reducing voter fraud in Florida, but critics loudly protested that the law's real intent was to discourage voters who are most likely to vote Democratic, such as welfare recipients, college students, and minorities, including African Americans and Hispanics. (See ELECTIONS AND VOTING RIGHTS, pages 67-70 for additional information.) Note also: Parts of this law are currently being adjudicated.

*In November 2011 the tragic and widely publicized death of a student at Florida A&M University (FAMU), the state's most notable black institution of higher learning, caused a spontaneous outcry against an epidemic of vicious hazing practices associated with the school's nationally acclaimed Marching 100 band. Robert Champion, a drum major with the band who was the latest in a long line of hazing victims, died from blunt force trauma from a beating on a band bus following a football game against rival Bethune-Cookman. Gov. Scott interjected himself into the case, strongly urging that FAMU's president, James Ammons, be suspended while the drum major's death and earlier hazing incidents were being investigated. However, university board members, offended by Scott's interference, refused to comply with his request. Later, FAMU students, angry about Scott's negative stance regarding President Ammons, marched to the Governor's Mansion on Adams Street in protest mode. Scott emerged with a bullhorn and tried to placate the students by telling them he cared about what happens to their university, and besides he knew what it was like to grow up disadvantaged in public housing. This only angered the students more, one of them shouting back at the insensitive governor, "We're NOT poor!" (Note to Gov. Scott: Floridians are tired of hearing about your deprived childhood in public housing. Please tell us more about how you got rich at Columbia/HCA.)

*In another more recent case involving the death a young black man, the governor's intervention proved to be somewhat more constructive. (See GUNS AND GUN CONTROL, pages 81-82 for information about the nationally explosive Trayvon Martin case involving Florida's controversial "stand your ground" law.)

*Just as Gov. Scott was winding up his first 16 months as governor, he "stepped in it" again when he traveled to Miami to sign a bill into law passed by the Legislature in its 2012 session that bans Florida state agencies from dealing with companies that do more than $1 million worth of business annually with Cuba or Syria. An unmistakable attempt to curry favor with Miami's Castro-hating, conservative Republican Cuban-American community, a politically influential minority in South Florida, Scott's mission turned sour very quickly after he left the bill-signing ceremony and issued a letter indicating the law he had just signed was unenforceable because it conflicted with federal law. Hopping mad, the Cuban-Americans took to their talk-radio and TV shows, threatening to sue the back-stabbing governor or, at the very least, force him drink a spiked mojito when they see him next!

OPEN GOVERNMENT AND PUBLIC RECORDS

Florida is justifiably proud of its strong open government laws, which date back to the 1960s. On the other hand, Rick Scott, who came to Florida government as a hard-driving businessman steeped in a culture of secrecy, found the notion of transparency and the public's right to know alien concepts. It's no surprise, then, that during the first months of his governorship, Scott treated the idea of government in the sunshine with contempt or that key staff members followed his lead. For instance, Mary Ann Carter, an early adviser to Scott, warned people who asked for her email address, "I rarely check and almost never respond to work email because of the open records law." Such an acknowledgement surprised open government advocates who wondered what the Scott administration had to hide? It wasn't long before the new governor had a new nickname: the Prince of Darkness.

Specific instances involving Scott's negative attitudes toward open government and access to public records are found in Chapter 5, pages 000, which deal with purged email messages and the censorship of ordinary citizens at a public meeting at The Villages; and Chapter 6, pages 000, where the Capitol Press Corps' access to public officials at an event in Tallahassee was the issue.

It should be reiterated here that when Scott brought Steve MacNamara on board as his chief of staff in July 2011, the governor began to soften his belligerent stance concerning the issue of open government as part of his image makeover. And by the end of 16 months as governor, Scott had apparently endorsed MacNamara's last image-enhancing proposal. Called Project Sunburst, it allows journalists and the public to access emails to and from Scott by 11 top members of his administration by searching the website flgov.com/sunburst. The once hostile governor won praise from the Florida press for allowing the people this glimpse into what goes on behind the governor's still frequently closed doors. The big question of course is, now that MacNamara has left the administration, would the Prince of Darkness return? There have been some indications that may occur.

PARKS

Florida's award-winning public parks system, which has been recognized nationally as the best in the country, is almost 80 years old. Currently it comprises 160 diverse parks that serve the recreational, educational, and environmental needs Floridians and visitors alike. The oldest parks were created in 1935 during the Great Depression by the Civilian Conservation Corps (CCC), and the newest are just a few years old. All help protect ecologically sensitive land and wildlife.

No one has ever tried to make serious money off the parks—that is until Gov. Scott and his mania for privatization took over the executive branch of Florida's government in January 2011. Early on, the profit-minded governor put out the word in hush-hush fashion to the state's top brass at the Division of Recreation and Parks (part of the Florida Department of Environmental Protection) that he wanted to turn over portions of 50 or more parks to private corporations for development, including designing, building, and operating large numbers of RV campsites and the various support facilities they require (e.g., "dump stations" and stormwater basins). The plan called for starting the privatization program at four major parks: De Leon Springs, Edward Ball Wakulla Springs, Fanning Springs, and Honeymoon Island.

It was the latter, Honeymoon Island State Park, the "crown jewel" of the Florida park system, that created a firestorm of criticism against the plan put forth by Scott and the park service. Located on a barrier island just north of the city of Dunedin on the Gulf Coast, Honeymoon Island has been a mecca for those interested in fishing, swimming, picnicking, and boating since it became a public park in the 1970s. In 2010, for instance, the park logged more than one million visitors. The island also offers diverse ecosystems from tidal marsh to pine forests. People became outraged when they learned about what was in the works for this popular natural destination. Creating the RV sites would entail cutting down trees, and of course the gopher tortoises and any other wildlife that might get the way of private enterprise would have to be relocated—if they survived.

Loud protests by organizations such as the Florida Audubon Society and the Florida Native Plant Society and hundreds of individual citizens caused Scott and his people to scrap their callous attempt to sell off parts of Honeymoon Island Park, at least for the time being. But word has it that budget cuts have forced many other state parks to accept privatizing some of their services. Craig Pittman reported in the *St. Petersburg Times* (July 16, 2011), "As of this month the state has handed over the job of running a lodge, a number of restaurants and gift shops, and one canoe and kayak rental operation over to private contractors."

Most recently the Legislature in its 2012 session weighed in on a related matter, passing a bill that would allow zoos to lease state land, including parkland, for the purpose of breeding exotic animals. Gov. Scott vetoed the the bill, claiming that he already as the authority to lease state-owned land.

PRISONS

The major issues: 1) Privatizing South Florida prisons; 2) Privatizing prisoners' healthcare; and 3) Prison closures.

PRIVATIZING SOUTH FLORIDA PRISONS: Among the most contentious issues that Gov. Scott confronted in the first 16 months of his four-year term involved the state's costly prison system, the third largest in the nation comprising nearly 150 facilities with an inmate population of well over 100,000. When campaigning for the governorship, Scott vowed eventually to cut $1 billion from the Florida Corrections Department's $3 billion annual budget. Scott's solution—by no means a new idea to those familiar with the problem of burgeoning costs in the corrections industry—entailed privatizing dozens of prisons and work camps in South Florida, a move that to be effective, the governor warned, had to produce a savings for the state of at least 7 percent a year, or roughly $16.5 million. The plan Scott proposed, and the Legislature debated, represented the most ambitious effort ever undertaken in the U.S. to privatize a large number of prisons all at same time.

Lawsuits, a conflict of interest complaint, political horse-trading, and strong-arm tactics by legislators and lobbyists all played a role in how the issue finally played out at the end of the 2012 legislative session. Here's a chronology of the salient events:

'In August 2011 Edwin Buss, Scott's newly appointed prison czar, was forced to resign, lasting only seven months, partly due to his support for a lawsuit filed by the Police Benevolent Association (PBA), the union representing Florida's prison guards and other corrections personnel, almost all of whom overwhelmingly opposed privatization.

'In September the Teamsters Union, battling to replace the PBA as the prison workers' union, slapped Scott with an ethics complaint, charging him with conflict of interest because he received $30,000 for his inaugural expenses from each of the country's two largest private prison contractors, Geo Group Inc. and Corrections Corp. of America. That suit appeared to go nowhere.

'In October 2011 Leon County Circuit Judge Jackie Fulford ruled the Legislature's attempt to privatize South Florida's prisons unconstitutional, the reason being legislators broke the law when they simply inserted the plan into the 2011-12 budget without a bill being introduced, considered via the committee process, or voted on by the Legislature. The judge make it clear that the law allows for privatization of prisons, but that the legislative leadership's furtive method of doing so violated Florida's Constitution. As a result, in January 2012 a bill to move forward on prison privatization in South Florida was introduced in the Florida Senate.

'In February 2012 state Sen. Mike Fasano, a Republican, was stripped of his chairmanship of the Florida Senate budget subcommittee because he opposed the plan to privatize prisons, citing a report that some 3,800 prison workers might lose their jobs. Later that month state Sen. Larcenia Bullard, a Democrat and another opponent of privatization who had been ill recently with a heart condition, was badgered and bullied by pro-privatization forces who desperately needed her vote in favor of the plan. Bullard was in tears at one point and needed sympathetic senators to extricate her from a committee room where she was being given the third degree by Republican Senate leaders and lobbyists.

'Finally, on February 14, near the end of the 2012 session, the normally servile Republican-controlled Florida Senate voted to defeat the privatization plan on a close bipartisan vote, 21-19, nine Republicans joining a dozen Democrats to vote no. The bill, had it passed, would have authorized privatizing 27 prisons and work camps in 18 counties in South Florida. It's a good bet that Scott and the privatization advocates will be back in the 2013 session.

PRIVATIZING PRISONERS' HEALTHCARE: Scott's other campaign pledge concerning prisons was to save money by outsourcing all types of medical care for prisoners—physical, mental, dental, prescription drugs, etc.—to private providers. This plan, which would apply to all 100,000-plus inmates in Florida prisons and work camps, was also never introduced, vetted in committee, debated, or voted on by the Legislature. Instead, like the original effort to privatize the South Florida prisons, it was simply sneaked into the budget, and before most legislators knew what had happened two out-of-state firms were hired to provide medical services at a cost savings to the state of 7 percent annually. Two unions—the Florida Nurses Association and the American Federation of State, County and Municipal Employees (AFSCME) argued the heathcare plan was unconstitutional and its implementation should be rescinded.

PRISON CLOSURES: Although the privatization issue very much dominated the agenda concerning Florida's prisons during Scott's first third of his term as governor, prison closures also stirred up some controversy, mostly about why this facility was targeted for closure when that one wasn't. For instance, why was Jefferson Correctional Institution in tiny Jefferson County (pop. 14,000) in the Florida Panhandle put on the list for extinction? Well, approximately half of the county's population is African American and politically it votes heavily Democratic, as Gov. Scott found out when he lost the county to Alex Sink by a landslide in November 2010. Another example: Why shutter the Hillsborough Correctional Institution in West Central Florida, an all-female prison and the only one in the system that is (or was) faith-based? Small with only 330 inmates, perhaps Scott didn't think the facility was pulling it weight money-wise? On the other hand, it has had many success stories about how female felons have turned around their lives thanks to the prison's faith and character programs. During 2011-12 only seven counties (of a total of 67) were directly affected by prison closings, which is why the issue usually does not get much statewide attention but rather is debated at the local level.

PROPERTY INSURANCE

Florida has always been a relatively inexpensive state to live in. There's no need for heavy winter clothes or pricey ski togs; there's no need for snow tires or ice fishing gear, etc. Likewise, as far as taxes are concerned, the place can be quite economical. There's no income tax—it's in the state's Constitution. Property taxes have gone up over the years, but compared with most other states these taxes remain reasonable, especially for people who have lived in their homes since the adoption of the "Save Our Homes" constitutional amendment in 1992. That addition to the Florida Constitution caps annual property tax increases at no more than 3 percent or the rate of inflation, whichever is lower. Florida does have a sales tax, first implemented in 1949 as a 3 percent "limited" tax, and predictably the percent has crept up and up over the years. Still, it's not out of line with the sales tax rate in most other states.

What is currently vexing Floridians is the rising cost of property insurance, which many have taken to calling a "hurricane tax." Homeowners who have a mortgage are required by lenders to buy property insurance, but even people who own their homes outright usually want the insurance in case calamity strikes. Even renters are hurt by any substantial increase in property insurance, which owners tend to pass on at least a portion of to their tenants.

There was a time not that long ago when Floridians were able to buy property insurance at moderate rates from any number of national or regional insurance carriers. However, beginning in the early 1990s with the especially devastating Hurricane Andrew in 1992, which was followed in 2004 and 2005 by a host of other destructive storms (i.e., Charley, Ivan, Frances, Jeanne, and Wilma), the major national insurance companies began doubling, tripling, and even quadrupling their rates and, when they didn't get everything they wanted, they began pulling out of Florida altogether, at least in the property insurance area. This led to the creation of Citizens Property Insurance Corp., a state-sponsored property insurer "of last resort" that was intended to provide coverage at affordable rates. At present the company is the state's largest property insurer, until recently writing approximately a thousand policies a day.

The problem is, as *Florida Trend* (January 2012) has pointed out, Citizens, with its traditional low rates, has never been "actuarially sound." In other words, "Citizens subjects the state to a financial catastrophe in the event of a big storm." Enter Gov. Scott, who indicated during his campaign for governor that the major private carriers (e.g., State Farm; Allstate) who abandoned Florida should be enticed to come back basically on their own terms: "We have to have a regulatory environment that they [the private companies] feel comfortable with, that they're going to get treated fairly, and we've got to make sure that they're financially viable"—that is, let the companies write the rules. Indeed Scott's solution would mean much higher premiums for Floridians, or as one wag put it, "The tax that now hurts the most isn't even called a tax." Most recently, Scott has pushed hard for Citizens to push its rates sky-high in an effort to entice the private companies back to Florida. Either way, property insurance costs will double or triple for Floridians in the near future, regrettably forcing untold numbers out of their homes.

PUBLIC CORRUPTION AND ETHICS IN GOVERNMENT

In recent years Florida has got a bad reputation when it comes to politics and politicians. Who can forget the hanging chads that symbolized the state's blunders in the 2000 presidential race between George W. Bush and Al Gore? Florida became "Flori-duh." In the more mundane area of local and state political corruption, Florida has also scored a great big fat "duh." Here's how former Gov. Bob Graham recently summarized the situation in an interview with *Florida Trend* (January 2012): "I don't think Floridians appreciate the ethical challenge that our state faces. The [U.S.] Department of Justice publishes a state-by-state list of public officials who have been convicted of some crime. Florida was not only No. 1, but there was a noticeable gap between No. 1 and No. 2. When you ask people what's the most corrupt state, they may say New Jersey. But we're here."

Need more evidence? In 2010 a statewide grand jury charged with looking into public corruption reported there is so much government malfeasance in Florida that citizens are literally being charged a "corruption tax." Moreover, the grand jury made a series of thoughtful suggestions about how to begin addressing some of the problems. Need more evidence? For five consecutive years Paula Dockery, a Republican state senator from Lakeland, has tried and failed to have the Florida Legislature adopt an ethics proposal that would prohibit legislators from voting on bills that might provide benefits for themselves, their families, their friends, or their employers. The fact that such a modest reform has been rejected by state lawmakers time and time again is simply scandalous.

Though Rick Scott didn't know much about Florida when he was elected governor, he did know about the widespread public corruption and unethical behavior that plagues the state. We know he knew because he pledged in his inaugural address in January 2011 to find ways to implement the aforementioned grand jury's recommendations. Everyone was pleased that Scott, a man who came to the governorship with a history in the area of shady dealings, would so quickly step up and publicly commit to try to change Florida's shameful culture of corruption. Then nothing. Months went by . . . . Silence . . . . Even the Tea Party, which looked upon Scott as a savior, was upset, one of its most vocal members complaining near the end of 2011, "I haven't heard him say one word on it." "It" of course referred to corruption and ethical lapses among Florida lawmakers and other public officials. So far, as of April 2012, nothing . . . .

PUBLIC EMPLOYEES AND THEIR PENSION FUND

It's not difficult to make the case that Gov. Scott, a private sector man through and through, doesn't much care for rank-and-file public employees. He made this very clear when as the newly elected governor he quickly laid off 3,500 state workers (with another 4,000 to go the following year). He also made it clear when he attempted to have most state workers subjected to periodic drug testing, and again when he pushed for legislation that would curtail the power of public employee unions, and again when he revealed his opposition to collective bargaining, and yet again when he cut the pay of practically all government workers in the state by forcing them to contribute a percentage of their salary to their pension fund—this while knowing full well that most Florida public employees had not had a pay raise in years.

Scott didn't get everything he wanted, but he got enough to make a lot of public sector enemies. Here's a bit of anecdotal corroboration: Soon after taking office, Scott toured various state agencies in and around Tallahassee, introducing himself and speaking briefly about each agency's mission, and then asking if anyone had questions. He rarely received any. When he got to the end of his visit at the state Corrections

Department, he politely asked for questions and, behold, one employee, an older woman, shocked him by asking one that was probably tougher than any he had received during the campaign: "You said to hold you accountable. State employees have seen, since the [Jeb] Bush administration, a reduction in state employees. I have been with this agency for many years. And I've seen where our staff has been significantly cut. We are required to do more with less. State employees haven't had a raise in five or six years. You're asking us to contribute to our pension plan and contribute more to our insurance. My question is simple: What have you required for the wealthiest Floridians to contribute to the state revenues?"

According to a reporter on the scene, the question received applause. Scott, however, had no answer, though he waffled on for seven minutes about capitalism, including references to Walmart, China, taxes in Illinois, and these words of wisdom: "If you work in the private sector, here's the things you have to do: Your overhead has to come down each and every year as a percentage of revenues. Every year. That has not happened in state government." Scott's answer received no applause. (See "Scott evades staff cuts query" in the *St. Petersburg Times*, February 23, 2011.)

Of all of the issues concerning public employees and the Scott administration, none is more sensitive—or momentous—than the future of the state's enormous pension fund, officially the Florida Retirement System (FRS). An incredible amount of money is involved. FRS is the fourth largest pension fund in the U.S. and is currently valued at roughly $121 billion. You can understand why Gov. Scott is interested. Likewise, at present there are more than 655,000 active employees in FRS, including teachers, police officers, firefighters, office personnel, janitors, and a multitude of other state and county workers. They too have a vested interest in the future of the fund, which is managed by Florida's State Board of Administration (SBA), which in turn is overseen by the state's governor, attorney general, and chief financial officer, who as a group act as trustees.

In the past FRS has been reasonably well managed, though some controversial investments have led to losses that have resulted in calls for increased accountability and transparency. During Scott's first 16 months in office, worse problems have occurred. The present executive director of SBA, Ash Williams, supported by Gov. Scott, repeatedly refused to make available public records dealing with questionable hedge fund investments totaling $125 million. Williams' most outrageous attempt at cover-up came when he relented and provided state Sen. Mike Fasano with the requested documents, but they were so heavily redacted that Fasano found "many of the records essentially useless." On top of that, Williams sent the senator a bill for $10,750.17 to cover the cost of retrieving and processing the documents! In addition, Williams has constantly lobbied to put more of FRS's pension money in risky "alternative" investments, which once was capped at 5 percent and recently has risen to 10 and now 20 percent. Why Williams' bosses—Gov. Scott, Attorney General Pam Bondi, and Chief Financial Officer Jeff Atwater—tolerate this sort of suspicious behavior by a man managing billions of dollars that belong to Florida workers should concern anyone and everyone who has a stake in FRS.

Meanwhile, Gov. Scott—equally well-known as Mr. Privatize—floated a plan to overhaul and eventually do away with FRS. It would 1) force current public workers in the system to pay a percentage of their salary into the fund, which would save the state considerably money; and 2) not allow new employees to join FRS, but instead urge them to create 401(k) retirement accounts offered by private investment companies. In time FRS would be phased out. In other words, workers would exchange a plan that offers a defined benefit (FRS) for one that requires a defined contribution.

In 2011 the Legislature eventually voted to require members of FRS to contribute 3 percent of their salary to the pension fund, and of course Scott immediately approved the bill. But in March 2012, in a thumping defeat for the governor and the lawmakers, Leon County Circuit Judge Jackie Fulford ruled the law "an unconstitutional taking of private property without full compensation . . . . To find otherwise would mean that a contract with our state government has no meaning and that the citizens of our state can place no trust in the work of our Legislature." The judge went on to point out that, in order to legally require employees hired before July 1, 2011 to contribute a portion of their salaries to FRS, contractual rights given the employees by the Legislature in 1974 would have to be renegotiated. Scott has appealed Judge Fulford's decision to the Florida Supreme Court.

TRANSPORTATION

The major issues: 1) High-Speed rail project Tampa to Orlando; 2) Central Florida SunRail commuter project; 3) Sale of state-owned airplanes; and 4) Auto Insurance reform.

HIGH-SPEED RAIL PROJECT TAMPA TO ORLANDO: Gov. Scott had been in office for merely a month and half when, on February 16, 2011, he killed the high-speed rail (or bullet train) project, a visionary, federally financed undertaking that would have provided the first of many links in a high-speed rail system eventually serving the entire nation. The $2.4 billion project would also have brought many well-paying construction and related jobs to Florida.

Scott's shocking decision, apparently based on a negative analysis by a right-wing think tank, the Reason Foundation, was roundly opposed by many political, business, and community leaders. The Florida Senate, which had earlier given thumbs up to the deal, composed a letter admonishing Scott for his unilateral action; the Senate also requested that the U.S. Department of Transportation give the state additional time to try to find a way around or to overturn the governor's unexpected decision.

On March 1, two state senators (a Republican and a Democrat) filed a lawsuit in the Florida Supreme Court seeking to force Scott to reverse himself and immediately approve the Tampa-to-Orlando rail project, their argument being the governor's veto was unconstitutional because he lacked the authority to refuse funds the Legislature had already approved. Scott's personal attorney, Charles Trippe, who had just been hired the day before, had never argued a case before the state's high court, but despite that and working with only a few hours sleep, he managed to convince the justices the governor had not violated the Florida Constitution.

Unfortunately, a golden opportunity was lost for Florida to have a leadership role in creating a national public high-speed rail system. In fact, some who were angered by Scott's decision believe it was prompted as much by the governor's vitriolic dislike for public enterprise and President Obama than it was for any economic reason. What's interesting here is that around this time the Florida Department of Transportation commissioned a study of the Tampa-Orlando project by two consulting firms, Wilbur Smith Associates and Steer, Davis, Gleave, both of which concluded the high-speed rail line, had it been constructed, "would have been a fiscally sound decision." Specifically, their report predicted the rail line "would have made an annual surplus of $31 million to $45 million within a decade of operation." Commenting on the study, Ross Capon, president of the National Association of Railroad Passengers, noted, "What's been lost is Florida's opportunity to raise it economic development image worldwide, along with an alternative transportation system for the state." Vision might be an overused word these days, but Scott's utter lack of it has cost Florida mightily.

The *Tampa Tribune* is credited with bringing the Florida DOT report to light after a lengthy and hard-fought public records request. (See "High-speed rail would have been profitable, state report says" by Ted Jackovics, TBO.com, February 6, 2012.)

CENTRAL FLORIDA SUNRAIL COMMUTER PROJECT: A few months after Scott shoot down the bullet train, he confronted another rail issue, this time whether or not to proceed with the construction of a 61.5-mile commuter train that would service Orlando and surrounding counties. In this case the cost of the project, estimated to be $1.3 billion, would be shared by state and local taxpayers, with the state picking up the tab for any operating losses during the first seven years after which local governments would assume that responsibility. The deal also called for the state to pay $432 million to CSX Corp., a Jacksonville-based freight rail operator, for SunRail's right to use CSX's tracks in the Orlando area. The state would also agree to make upgrades to CSX's infrastructure elsewhere in Florida, and it would be liable for any accidents that might occur on the shared tracks, even if CSX was at fault. No wonder knowledgeable people were calling this a "sweetheart deal" for both CSX and Orlando, or that Alex Sink, then Florida's chief financial officer, issued warnings about the potentially high cost of liability claims against the state.

Other critics of the plan—and there were many, especially those who felt Scott had shafted the people of Florida by saying no to the federally financed Tampa-Orlando project—loudly called for the governor to reject the Central Florida commuter train on the basis of cost alone. As Lakeland Republican state Sen. Paula Dockery put it, "When the SunRail/CSX commuter project is viewed from a purely business vantage point, the project falls so far below what a savvy business owner would accept that it is somewhat baffling."

Again Scott, who seems to enjoy the attention being perverse brings, did the unexpected thing and approved SunRail. The man who inspired countless lawsuits defended his decision by saying he might be sued if he killed SunRail.

SALE OF STATE-OWNED AIRPLANES: On the campaign trail in 2010, candidate Scott burnished his credentials as a cost-cutter by pledging to sell Florida's two airplanes—a 2000 King Air 350 and a 2003 Cessna Citation Bravo—if elected governor. And as soon as he assumed the office he immediately did that. No more "Air Florida," which had been used principally as a time-saver for top government officials to conduct business around the state. When all was said and done, the state saved more than $2 million, which was the annual cost of operating the planes, plus it gained another $560,000 from the sale of the planes after paying off $3.4 million still owed on the Cessna.

Scott, of course, had his own private jet to fly around in, but what about his cabinet officers and key legislators? They didn't own airplanes like Daddy Warbucks Scott. And it must said for the benefit of anyone unfamiliar with Florida geography, that Tallahassee is one of the the most out-of-the-way capital city in the U.S., located in the

Panhandle closer to Georgia and Alabama than any Florida major city. Some wondered about the possibility that Scott had ulterior motives when he sold the planes: Did he want to keep people like Adam Putnam, currently the state's agriculture commissioner and a man often mentioned as a future Florida governor, from using state planes to go here and there promoting themselves and their political aspirations? Maybe Scott had sold the planes so he would be the only person who could jet around the state at a moment's notice, being Ricky on the spot in any crisis situation? The official answer from a spokesperson: No, Gov. Scott does not have a "Machiavellian political approach to things."

AUTO INSURANCE REFORM: In its 2012 session the Florida Legislature passed and Gov. Scott signed legislation that overhauled the state's mandatory no-fault auto insurance law, the main objectives being 1) to bring down the cost of premiums, and 2) to reduce an epidemic of fraudulent personal injury claims that is estimated to cost Floridians in the neighborhood of $1 billion annually. Comprehensive reform of the state's personal injury protection (PIP) law had been one of Scott's top priorities, and since passage of the reform bill he has developed a campaign-style TV commercial featuring himself gushing about new aspects of the law.

Major changes in the law, most of which don't take effect until January 1, 2013, include these provisions: 1) Accident victims must be treated within 14 days; 2) Only victims with "emergency medical conditions" will be eligible to receive the full $10,000 PIP benefit; 3) Only medical doctors, osteopathic physicians, dentists, physician assistants, or advanced registered nurse practitioners will be authorized to determine if a victim has an emergency medical condition; 4) Nonemergency victims will be eligible for only $2,500 for PIP treatment; 5) Chiropractors will be allowed to treat victims, but PIP will no longer pay for acupuncture or massage therapy; 6) Insurance companies will be allowed to question policyholders under oath when investigating fraud cases; and 7) In some cases attorneys' fees may be limited.

Opponents of the reform legislation make the point that insurance companies will now be able to limit PIP claims to $2,500 if a serious injury is not diagnosed with 14 days—but it's common knowledge that many types of serious auto injuries (e.g., to neck, back, and spine) don't always become apparent within a short arbitrary period of time such as 14 days. Also missing from the legislation is a provision that auto insurers must lower their rates. Despite such criticism, Gov. Scott and the Florida Legislature have appeared to score a short-term political victory with their auto insurance reform legislation.

APPENDIX 2

A BRIEF LOOK AT THE FLORIDA LEGISLATURE IN 2011 AND 2012

First, some basic facts about the Florida Legislature:

*As in the federal system, Florida government is divided into three branches: legislative, executive, and judicial. Again like the federal system, the Florida Legislature (hereafter just plain Legislature) is bicameral, that is it has two houses, Senate and House of Representatives.

*The Florida Legislature currently has a total of 160 elected members, 40 in the Senate and 120 in the House.

*Members of both houses have term limits. A senator can be elected to no more than two 4-year terms in succession and a house member can be elected to no more than four 2-year terms in succession. However, term-limited members of either house can run again after being out of office for two years. Likewise a term-limited member may run for a different seat in either the House or Senate without waiting two years.

*The Legislature meets in regular session for 60 days at the beginning of the year. The governor of Florida has the power to call members into special session anytime later in the year to consider one or more urgent issues. This power is usually used sparingly.

*The Legislature's main responsibility is to produce a balanced budget for the fiscal year. The budgetary year begins July 1 and ends the following year on June 30. Florida's governor also prepares a budget, which is sent to the Legislature for its consideration. The Legislature, however, has the final word on the budget.

*Power in the Legislature is concentrated in the hands of just a few leaders, such as the president of the Senate, chair of the Senate Budget Committee, and Speaker of the House. Members who do not support leadership's positions do so at their peril.

*In addition to the Legislature's 160 members, there are approximately 2,000 registered lobbyists—or about a dozen lobbyists for each elected member—circulating when the lawmakers are in session. More than a few of the lobbyists are former members of the Florida House or Senate, who are busy working on behalf of various special interests, which sometimes includes actually writing legislation.

What follows is brief commentary on the two sessions (2011 and 2012) Gov. Scott interacted with during his first 16 months as governor.

For many years conservative Democrats from northern Florida, mockingly called the Pork Chop Gang, controlled the Legislature. In recent years conservative Republicans, including Tea Party folk, have taken control of the legislative branch of Florida's government. Republicans have had majorities in both houses since 1996. Having strong conservative, pro-business allies in the Legislature has proved to be a boon to Gov. Scott and his policies. Rarely have he and the legislative leadership knocked heads. If when elected Scott had had a more liberal Legislature, he almost certainly could not have got away with many of his highly questionable actions. In a word, the Legislature in 2011 and 2012 tended to act as his handmaiden.

Because the Florida Legislature is very much a part-time body, meeting only 60 days a year, plus the occasional special session, more and more of the House and Senate's responsibilities are gradually being turned over to the governor and his staff, which are on duty year around. The Legislature simply doesn't have the time or the manpower to do the nitty-gritty legislative work required by a state as large and complex as Florida. Examples: Recently the Legislature has given the governor power to supervise agency rule-making; power to offer millions of dollars to out-of-state companies to relocate to Florida; and power to remove questionable members of local job agencies funded by the state. These and many similar governmental obligations were carried out by the Legislature until recently. One Democratic representative got so exercised about this trend that he blurted out, "Why don't we just change the title of governor to king and give him a crown and be done with it?" Of course another, more practical suggestion is why not change the Florida Constitution and have a full-time Legislature?? After all, Florida—the nation's fourth largest state, soon to be the third largest—has an annual budget of $70 billion. North Carolina, for example, has a full-time Legislature and a budget less than half that of Florida's.

Another problem that plagues the Florida Legislature are term limits, which thrust inexperienced members into positions of near-absolute power for a short time. Often the results are appalling. A recent example is the farce created by JD Alexander and the establishment of Florida Polytechnic University. Term limits also permit lobbyists to achieve excessive power—lobbyists remain while elected legislators are here today and gone tomorrow. And finally term limits tend to breed lawmakers who are sometimes more interested in what's in it for themselves than how they can contribute to making Florida a better place to live. An example: In the 2012 session, the Senate Budget Committee debated the issue of why legislators should pay a lot less for their health insurance than most Floridians, including rank-and-file state workers. One courageous senator, Joe Negron, a Republican from Stuart, proposed to increase legislators' premiums from $8 to $50 a month for individual coverage and from $30 to $180 a month for family coverage. The proposal was defeated on an unrecorded voice vote.

Perhaps the moral here is Rick Scott and the current Florida Legislature deserve one another.

AUTHOR'S NOTE

SOURCES AND REFERENCES

Great Scott is not intended as a scholarly treatise, but rather is a broadside written in response to a political moment in time. The book therefore is not festooned with footnotes or an extensive bibliography of sources consulted.

I do want to note, however, that *Florida Trend,* a scrupulously edited magazine devoted broadly to the business of Florida, has been especially valuable as a source. In addition to its monthly print issues, *Trend* provides subscribers with a daily online service that references pertinent articles, news stories, and opinion pieces about Florida from a host of both print and electronic publications.

Citations to significant quoted material in the book are included in the text. Other quoted material and all factual information can be verified, should it be necessary, by searching the Internet by subject. Of course, as is well-known, the Internet contains true facts, questionable facts, and lies masquerading as facts. For that reason I have made every effort to use only sources with a proven reputation for accuracy and credibility.

Ken Kister

NAME AND SUBJECT INDEX

V

Vandewater, David. 18
Villages (The), 40, 47
voting. voting rights. and voter suppression,
    see elections and voting rights

W

Walt Disney Company, 78
water and water management districts
    (WMDs), 72-75
welfare recipients. 62-63, 92
Wilbur Smith Associates, 103
Wiles. Susie. 25-26, 39
Williams. Ash, 101-02
Wynn Resorts, 78

Y

Yerrid, Steve, 76

Z

Zimmerman, George, 81
zoos, 96

CPSIA information can be obtained at www.ICGtesting.com
Printed in the USA
LVOW06s0009260713

344657LV00001B/243/P